Sketch of the Official Life of John A. Andrew, as Governor of Massachusetts, Etc. With a Portrait.
by Albert Gallatin Browne

125

10881. aa 31

# SKETCH OF THE OFFICIAL LIFE

OF

# JOHN A. ANDREW,

## AS GOVERNOR OF MASSACHUSETTS,

TO WHICH IS ADDED THE

VALEDICTORY ADDRESS OF GOVERNOR ANDREW, DELIVERED
UPON RETIRING FROM OFFICE, JANUARY 5, 1866, ON
THE SUBJECT OF RECONSTRUCTION OF THE
STATES RECENTLY IN REBELLION.

NEW YORK:
PUBLISHED BY HURD AND HOUGHTON.
Cambridge: Riverside Press.
1868.

To

# GENERAL U. S. GRANT,

*THIS SKETCH OF THE OFFICIAL LIFE OF ONE WHO*
*WAS HIS FRIEND, AND WHOSE FRIEND HE WAS;*
*AND THIS EDITION OF THE VALEDICTORY*
*ADDRESS OF GOVERNOR ANDREW, ARE,*
*BY PERMISSION, RESPECTFULLY*
*INSCRIBED.*

——◆——

"The tendency of the hour is towards Grant. And that is best. It is not the ideal good. It is bad for the country that he must leave his present post, — bad for him, the soldier, to try and to endure the hard fate which awaits him, in civil life. But it is the apparently *best practical good* the country can have. And Grant is so square and honest a man that I believe he is bound to be right in the main, anywhere." — GOVERNOR ANDREW, *October* 27, 1867, *three days before his death.*

# PREFACE.

THE following sketch comprises an article which appeared in the " North American Review " for January, 1868, and now is reprinted at the request of many friends of the late Governor Andrew, who desire to possess it in a separate form. To it now are added full copies of correspondence and documents to which the necessary limits of the former publication then permitted only brief reference. Use has also been made of other articles concerning Governor Andrew which have appeared since this was originally prepared ; chiefly, of one (the only defect of which is its brevity) written by his pastor, James Freeman Clarke, and printed in the February number of " Harper's Magazine." In every instance in which the words or facts of others are thus employed, due credit has been given to them by name.

This book has no pretension to the character of a full biography of Governor Andrew. Such a biography, at the request of the family of the Governor, is now in course of preparation by the experienced and accomplished hands of Mr. Edwin P. Whipple, whose work cannot fail to become of standard value in the literature and history of New England. The only merit to which the present writer lays claim, is that of personal and intimate knowledge of the facts which he has recorded in the following sketch ; hastily and imperfectly, no doubt, for it has been prepared during the few hours which he could spare from professional duties, but in such a manner, nevertheless, as he hopes may entitle it to friendly regard from those at whose request it has been written.

To it is added the valedictory address of Governor Andrew to the General Court of Massachusetts, upon retiring from office ; the sentiments and logic of which he maintained, without qualification, to the day of his death ; and by which he expressed a wish that his title to fame in the history of his country should be determined. The political issues of the war have produced no speech or essay on the subject of the reconstruction of the Rebel States more wise and humane and statesmanlike, or more worthy to be studied by the people of every section of the country on the eve of the presidential contest of the present year.

The photographer of the likeness of the Governor, which precedes the title-page, is Mr. Geo. K. Warren of Cambridgeport, Mass.

ALBERT G. BROWNE, Jr.
{ *Military Secretary to Governor*
*Andrew during the War.*

Boston, *April,* 1868.

# CONTENTS.

———◆———

CHAPTER IV.

CHAPTER V.

# SKETCH

## OFFICIAL LIFE OF GOVERNOR ANDREW.

———•———

## CHAPTER I.

The position of Governor Andrew in the history of Massachusetts. — His parentage, birth, school days, and college course. — Professional study with Mr. Fuller. — Admission to the Suffolk Bar. — His own expression of the duties, privileges, and opportunities of the young men of America, in their relation to their country.

THE traveller approaching Boston by the Providence Railroad traverses, nine miles from the city, a beautiful plain, through which wanders the slender stream of the Neponset among rich meadows studded with noble elms. In the background rise the piny slopes of the Blue Hill of Milton. From its ridges the climber looks eastward far out on the broad Bay of Massachusetts, beyond the capital and the islands of its harbor; and westward, over line upon line of swelling hills, each succeeding range fading in a fainter purple. Here and there rise higher sum-

mits, like Monadnock. By daylight, on the
nearer ranges are seen the roofs of a hundred
towns, the points of innumerable steeples, the
shafts of countless chimneys of busy factories.
By night, the factory buildings glitter like illu-
minated palaces, while the dwellinghouses clus-
tered in the villages shine with a steadier and
more homely glow. As the sun sinks behind
Wachusett into the Connecticut, brilliant gleams
flash over the sea from the lighthouses of the
Great Brewster and Minot's Ledge. More than
half of the million people of Massachusetts dwell
within the boundaries of that landscape.

In the centre of the plain stand long rows of
rough wooden barracks. The military precision
of their order discloses unmistakably their former
use. One half of them are now empty and
rotting in the Spring rains. The other half are
overflowing with an Irish tenantry, some ardent
speculator having bought them all in hope of
developing a permanent village from so unprom-
ising a nucleus.

Soon the railroad train leaves Readville and its
camp-ground in the distance, and shelters itself
at Boston in a station from which the passenger
steps out upon the old parade-ground of the
Common. Innocent players of base ball and
cricket have trodden off the turf in patches, until

the half bare ground looks like the well-worn covering of some ancient trunk. Over the elms and lindens swells the dome of the State House. In the western wing of the building, in front of the windows of the Council Chamber, painters are at work, on swinging platforms. Within, carpenters and masons are busy with plane and trowel. Soon, in the remodeling, all trace of the old apartments will be lost. The last Legislature even threatened the destruction of the whole building; and, if its history is to end in our day, perhaps then was the fit time. It began with the great Governor who, on the 19th of April, 1775, uttered the exulting cry, " O, what a glorious morning ! " and it well might end with him who had the fortune and the courage to repeat that cry with equal exultation, on the 19th of April, 1861. When the Readville Camp was last noisy with soldiery, and the parade-ground of the Common was dark with blue lines of regiments returned from real war, council was last held in that old Chamber by the greatest of the twenty successors of Samuel Adams.

Let it now change, like the camp and the once green parade. To the new era of Peace all the " modern improvements," which architect and carpenter and mason are making in the old building, fitly belong. So also to a new era belongs the enterprise of the speculator, to change into a peaceful hamlet the barracks where the great Governor of our modern day organized a hundred thousand Massachusetts soldiers for the war; and on the parade-ground, where they passed him in review, the school-boy playing with his ball and wicket is a fit representative of the new times. But, however great these changes, this generation must wholly pass away before the traveller crossing the Readville Plain, or the loiterer under the elms of the Charles Street Mall, or the visitor to the halls of the State Government, shall cease to recall and associate with the scene the figure and the face of Governor Andrew.

John Albion Andrew, the twenty-first Governor of the Commonwealth of Massachusetts, was born at Windham, a small town near Lake Sebago, about fifteen miles from Portland, May 31, 1818, two years before the organization of Maine as a separate State. He died at Boston, October 30, 1867. The family was English in origin, descending in America from Robert Andrew, who immigrated to Rowley Village, now Boxford, in Essex County, Massachusetts, and died there in 1668. It was connected by marriage with several of the famous ancient families of the Colony, — a grandmother of the Governor being a granddaughter of the brave Captain William Pickering, who commanded the Province Galley in 1707, to protect the fisheries against the French and Indians, and the mother of her husband being Mary Higginson, a direct descendant from Francis Higginson, the organizer of the first church in the Colony. A portrait of this old clergyman, his ancestor, depicted with snow-white hair and gray moustache, clad in a black robe, holding a book in one hand, on the index finger of which a large signet-ring is displayed, hung over the mantel on the chimney of the Council Chamber during the whole of Governor Andrew's administration. The grandfather of the Governor, whose name he bore, was a silversmith, and afterwards a successful merchant in the old and wealthy city of Salem. He removed to Windham, and died there in 1791. His son Jonathan was born in Salem, and lived there until manhood, when he, too, went to Windham, and married Nancy G. Pierce, a teacher in the Fryeburg Academy, where Daniel Webster also was once a teacher. She died in 1832; and soon afterwards he removed to Boxford, where he died in 1849. The Governor was their oldest son.

He was a school-boy at Windham and at Salem, and then a student in Bowdoin College. Of his college life Mr. Peleg W. Chandler spoke as follows in his felicitous eulogy at the Suffolk Bar meeting, held on November 4, 1867, after the Governor's death : —

"He took no rank as a scholar, and seemed to have not the slightest ambition for academical distinction ; he had no part at Commencement. This rosy, chub-faced boy, genial, affectionate, and popular, gave no indications of future renown, or of that ability, energy, and breadth of view for which he is now so celebrated. He was not regarded as dull, very much the contrary ; but he seemed to be indifferent to the ordinary routine of college honors, possessed of that happy temperament which enabled him then and for many years afterwards to pass quietly along without a touch of the carking cares and temptations that wait on the ambitious aspirations of the young as well as the old."

Immediately after graduating at college in the class of 1837, he came to Boston to study law, and prepared for the profession in the office of Henry H. Fuller, an uncle of Margaret Fuller. Of the relation between master and pupil, Mr. Chandler said : —

"It always seemed to me that his character was much affected by contact with that somewhat remarkable and much misunderstood lawyer. Mr. Fuller was a man of most genial temperament, an excellent scholar (second in the class of which Edward Everett was first), of wide reading and extensive acquirements; a man who loved young men, and aided and assisted them in every way he could; and also of such marked peculiarities, of such wonderful crotchets and such heroic obstinacy, that he naturally and especially attracted, and in some respects almost fascinated, his pupil. The attraction was mutual; they became almost like brothers. The student sat at the same office table with the master, entered into all the business affairs, wrote letters from dictation, and they seemed in fact like one person. Mr. Fuller had an extensive acquaintance with all sorts of men. He knew the personal history of almost every citizen of the town; and of all public characters, living and dead, he had a decided opinion, which he never hesitated to pronounce on any suitable occasion. Mr. Andrew, with the curiosity of a young man fresh from the country, took this all in; but what is remarkable, while some of the peculiar traits of the master stuck to the pupil, the latter had decided opinions of his own, especially in regard to American slavery, which were sometimes in ludicrous contrast with those of his senior. Mr.

Fuller was a conservative of conservatives. He stood by the ancient ways, even in the cut of his coat and the shape of his hat; his ruffled shirt and white cravat were significant of a past generation. Mr. Andrew soon became interested in many of the reform movements of the day, and was as firm and as peculiar in one direction as his friend was in another."

Then followed twenty years of steady practice at the Suffolk Bar, to which he was admitted in 1840. It was not a conspicuous career, but in it his biographer will find the marks of all the great qualities he afterwards displayed in office; for never was a life more consistent. In after years, in 1864, then at the height of his renown as Governor, he found time, even among the harassing cares of office, to prepare and deliver to the class graduating from the Medical School of Harvard College, their valedictory address, into which he condensed much of the philosophy of living which was matured in his own mind during this long term of patient professional labor.

"In no community in the world," said he, "is there brighter promise for competent young men than there is here; for the sphere is so vast, the ways are all open, and all possibilities are free to all men. It is only necessary that a young man of education should be willing to serve faithfully, to waste no time in dreams and passionate longings, but to make the most of himself by being useful and by proving his capacity, as occasions naturally occur. His time will surely come. There is never a surplus of competent and trustworthy men. They are always in request. Places are always in waiting for them. But the men themselves do not always at the right time appear."

" There is nothing more practically and simply true than that success, abiding and secure, the happiness and usefulness of a professional career, is proportioned to the purity, singleness, and generosity of the purpose with which it is pursued. No thinking man has lived to middle age who has not seen, with his own eyes, brilliant powers thrown away, capacity for lasting impression on society and for solid happiness as the reward of real good accomplished, made the forfeit of the poor and selfish pursuit of changeful Fortune, or uncertain Fame, or inglorious Ease. What a defeat is such a life! Will you treat your profession as a trade out of which merely to make your bread, while you indulge every whim or fancy of a mind to which duty is irksome and fruitful toil a mere fatigue? Then you sacrifice the hope of honorable competence, of solid reputation, the sweet and infinite satisfactions of a worthy life. Will you use it as the mere instrument of sordid gain ? Then you sacrifice your love for Science, who stands waiting to feed you with immortal food, and to open the rich storehouse of all her truth, while you dwarf your soul to the worship of the very dust she treads under her feet. Will you make your profession only a stepping-stone to preferment ? Then you strangle the spiritual and intellectual progeny which might bless your declining age, in order to reign for a while the heartless, aimless pretender of an hour, in a hollow and deceitful prosperity.

" The solicitude with which we naturally contemplate the future, if it does not degenerate into weak anxiety, is not unreasonable. The desire of excellence is not wholly to be disconnected from a sense of the value of other men's good opinion. A certain yearning for a proper sphere for generous ambition, a true appreciation of the rewards of meritorious effort, a manly tone of self-respect, are all, of course, desirable, nor are they, in any sense, unworthy. But when one sees so many great and good things waiting to be done, lying unaccomplished only for want of the men of faith, patience, intellect, and action; when we consider the vastness and variety of opportunity opening to the young men of America, who have really fitted themselves to serve their country and do their part in strengthening or enriching it, who are willing to buckle on their armor and contend for a brave mastery ; I think it seems as if self-interest, even, advises only that they should do justice to their own capacities and the means lying open before them, throw aside all weakness and all narrowness, and be faithful to themselves, generous to mankind, considering how bountiful is the Divine Providence to them. There is a margin for mistake and misadventure, for which all of us must allow. But it is usually and on the whole but a margin only. We must be willing to accept our mischances, and even our own errors, reckoning them for what in truth they are to courageous, persevering men, as illustrations of the limitations of everything which is simply human and not supernatural.

" Gentlemen, as citizens of a country larger than Europe, possessing elements of greater wealth and greater power than Europe, of capacity to feed and support a population exceeding the present numbers of the human race, you have only to develop yourselves and to apply your own powers and acquirements. The first duty of the citizen is to regard himself as made for his country, not to regard his country as made for him. If he will but subordinate his own self-hood, his own ambition, enough to perceive how great is his country and how infinitely less is he, is it not manifest that he presently becomes a sharer in her glory, a partaker of her greatness? He is strengthened by her strength, and inspired by her intellectual and moral life. While he contributes his little to the grand treasury of her various wealth of power and possession, he draws therefrom vigor and support with every breath he breathes. Standing utterly alone, what man is anything? But associated with his fellows, he receives the instruments, the means, the opportunities, and the facilities for action."

# CHAPTER II.

Professional career. — Training in public law. — Testimony as a
witness before the Congressional Committee of Investigation
into John Brown's attack on Harper's Ferry. — Theory of duty
towards unpopular causes. — Experience in cases of domestic relations. — Professional generosity. — Philanthropic services. —
Devotion to the Anti-Slavery cause. — Conservative constitution
of his mind. — Association with the religious society of James
Freeman Clarke. — Letter to Mr. Garrison. — Abstinence from
political office. — Service as State Representative in 1859. — He
leads the Legislature. — He declines a judicial appointment. —
Nomination for Governor. — Sympathy with John Brown. — Its
influence in the campaign. — His election. — His share in the
Chicago Convention of 1860. — His inaugural address as Governor. — His theory of the main issue involved in the rebellion.

IN the latter years of his professional practice
before becoming Governor, he was engaged in a
remarkable succession of cases involving high
questions of constitutional law. In 1854 he defended the parties indicted at Boston for rescuing
the fugitive slave Burns; in 1855 he defended
the British Consul at Boston against the charge
of violating our neutrality laws during the Cri-
mean War; in 1856 he argued the petition for a
writ of *habeas corpus* to test the legality of the
imprisonment of the Free State officers of Kansas

at Topeka.   More lately, in 1859, he initiated
and directed the measures for the legal defense
of John Brown in Virginia ; and in 1860 he was
of counsel for Francis B. Sanborn, at his discharge by the Supreme Court of Massachusetts
from the custody of the United States Marshal,
by whom he had been arrested on a warrant
from the Vice-President of the United States to
compel his appearance before the Congressional
Committee of Investigation into the affair at
Harper's Ferry.

He had himself appeared before that Committee as a witness on February 9, of the same year,
and been subjected to an examination conducted
chiefly by Jefferson Davis, then Senator from
Mississippi, and Senator Mason of Virginia, as
to his motives for taking so much trouble and
expense in John Brown's behalf.   In the light
of the subsequent career of his examiners some
of their questions and his answers have a peculiar
significance after the eight intervening years.*

---

* The following are extracts from the official report of his examination : —

"By the Chairman, Mr. Mason.   *Question*.   Will you state, sir,
whether your reason for volunteering your aid in this matter, and
the representations that you made to others, or what induced you
to act as you state you did act, was founded on the impression that
Brown was not going to have a fair or just trial, or was it founded
on a disposition to aid in his defense, because of his career against
the institution of slavery?

On his theory of duty as a lawyer, he never hesitated to defend unpopular and even odious causes. In illustration, besides his defense of the

"*Answer.* Well, sir, I know —

"*Question.* In other words, if you had no impressions that the trial was not one fairly and properly conducted, would you have acted as you did, in getting money for his defense, only from a desire to serve him because of the career in which he was embarked?

"*Answer.* I am quite clear on that point, putting the question in that way. As you, sir, first proposed the question, it was a little complex and intricate. Had I felt that Captain Brown and his associates were in the way to a full and complete opportunity for a fair judicial investigation into all their rights according to the laws of the jurisdiction within which they were, I have no reason to suppose that I should have interfered. I should have felt that I had no occasion to interfere. I had known about old Mr. Brown for several years, and I approved a great deal which I had heard of touching his career in Kansas; I thought he had been an honest, and conscientious, and useful assistant of the Free State cause. My impression of him was derived from many sources. I had never seen him but once in my life, and then only for a few moments. I' say in frankness that I felt a certain sympathy for a man who had, as I thought, been useful in behalf of a great cause in which I was interested. I had no sympathy with his peculiar conduct touching which he was then indicted. I felt injured by that, personally, as a Republican.

"*Question.* Suppose the only difficulty connected with his trial, as you heard, had been the want of means, would you and your friends then have volunteered to furnish the means to employ counsel?

"*Answer.* It is not easy, Mr. Chairman, for one man to speak as to another's motives. I can only speak as to my own; and you have now put a question which embarrasses me to this extent: It is unpleasant for a man to blow the trumpet of his own virtue, and I am sorry to be asked to state to what extent I may be a benevolent man, or otherwise. I can only give you one little circumstance, as

British Consul, may be named his advocacy of
Burnham, in 1860, against the inquisition of the
Massachusetts Legislature, and also his defense
in the United States courts, the same year, of

an illustration of what I might do under such circumstances. Last
year a man was convicted in Boston for piracy, and sentenced to
be hanged. I had never seen him, to speak to him, in my life, nor
did I know by sight any person related to him in any way. After
other efforts had been made, I devoted some weeks, at least, to
preparation, and came to Washington, at my own expense, without
fee or reward, or the hope of any, in order to press upon the Attorney
General and the President those considerations which I deemed
proper to be considered in support of the application for executive
clemency. The man's life was saved. I never spoke to him until
I accompanied Mr. Marshal Freeman to his cell, and assisted in the
reading of the President's warrant of commutation. I have sometimes done just such things as that on other occasions. I do not
profess to be a particularly benevolent man, but I mention that as
an illustration of what I *might* do, even for a stranger."

In answer to further questions the witness said : —

" I think that Captain Brown's foray into Virginia was a fruit of
the Kansas tree. I think that he and his associates had been educated up to the point of making an unlawful, and even unjustifiable, attack upon the people of a neighboring State — had been
taught to do so, and educated to do so by the attacks which the
Free State men in Kansas suffered from people of the slaveholding
States. And, since the gentleman has called my attention again
to that subject, I think the attack which was made against representative government in the assault upon Senator Sumner in Washington, which, so far as I could learn from the public press, was, if
not justified, at least winked at throughout the South, was an act
of very much greater danger to our liberties and to civil society
than the attack of a few men upon neighbors over the borders of a
State. I suppose that the State of Virginia is wealthy and strong,
and brave enough to defend itself against the assaults of any unorganized unlawful force.

" *Mr. Davis.* The sympathy which you say you expressed or

the notorious slaver-yacht Wanderer against forfeiture. In questions of domestic relations perhaps no member of our bar had a more extensive practice, or made deeper study of the law. His mind thus was busy always with the higher problems of philosophic jurisprudence, and his course of practice led him to comprehend thoroughly the mutual relations of the government and the people in all questions of personal liberty, so that when, in mature life, he was called to be Governor, he was already a well-trained political philosopher.

Much might be written of the cheerful kindness with which his professional skill and experience were always at the service of the poor. The writer of one of the notices of his life has truly said : —

felt towards John Brown, is that which you felt for a soldier engaged in such a civil war as that which you describe in Kansas.

" *The Witness.* That would hardly be a fair statement of my feeling.

" *Mr. Davis.* I wish merely to get what your feeling is. It is not a statement, but an inquiry.

" *The Witness.* I am constitutionally peaceable, and by opinion very much of a peace man, and I have very little faith in deeds of violence, and very little sympathy with them except as the extremest and direst necessity. My sympathy, so far as I sympathized with Captain Brown, was on account of what I believed to be heroic and disinterested services in defense of a good and just cause, and in support of the rights of persons who were treated with unjust aggression."

" Whoever had no other friend found it easy to appeal to his generosity. He showed this at the bar, where more than once he took up causes which hardly another lawyer would have touched, because otherwise the individual would have had no advocate and no hearing. At a time when the counsel for the wife in a divorce case was pretty sure to be paid less than the actual expenses of court, he was counsel for the wife in innumerable cases. The amount of his gratuitous professional services during his twenty years of practice will probably never be known. Certain it is that had he received full fees in all of them, he would not have been forced after five years of most distinguished official services, to return to the toil and drudgery of the bar in order to support his family."

And much also might be said of his service with organized philanthropic associations during this long period of twenty years — for which, however, this is not the place. The records of the societies for the amelioration of prison discipline, for the care of convicts after discharge from confinement, for the abolition of capital punishment, for the reform of inebriates, for the protection of sailors, for the promotion of peace ; and of numerous others of kindred nature ; bear testimony to the fidelity with which he served as a friend those who, except for him and such as he, were friendless.

From boyhood, he was devoted to the Anti-Slavery cause, and was an ally of all its champions, no matter by what political names they styled themselves or were styled by others. But the constitution of his mind was not destructive. He never believed in pulling down any valuable institution, because it was perverted to be a shelter for wrong, without first seeking if it could not be purged of the wrong and preserved with a value added by the purging.

His pastor, and close and constant friend, James Freeman Clarke, with whose religious society he associated himself soon after he came to Boston, has recorded a characteristic example of the application of this disposition to a dispute which occurred in the society, in 1845, in consequence of an exchange of pulpits with Theodore Parker. A part of the members had threatened to secede for that reason, and in the debate which followed this threat, the Governor, then a young man of twenty-seven, made a speech which Mr. Clarke describes as " seeming at the time as powerful in argument and persuasive in appeal as any I ever heard." The chief charge against Theodore Parker being that, as he rejected the supreme authority of the Bible, he could not properly be regarded as a Christian minister, the Governor cited the examples of the Roman Catholics, the Quakers, and the Swedenborgians, in denial of the validity of the charge ; and argued, moreover, that the Unitarian church did not make faith in the Scripture its foundation, but faith in Christ, however known.

" Finally," says Mr. Clarke, " he pleaded that the true way to treat all whom we supposed to be in error was not to go from them, but to go to them ; not shut them out, but take them in. Nor was it the right way, he contended, to leave a church because the majority conscientiously differed from us, but to remain in it and convince them. We never can do so much good by going only with those who agree with us ; for if only those who agree together go together, each party in the church hardens itself in its own opinions, and truth and error never come in contact."

At last, said he, in closing : " Brethren ! I do not believe in the principle of come-outer-ism. I am not a come-outer. I am a stay-iner. I shall not leave this church because the majority may differ from me on this or other questions. You may, indeed, turn me out ; but you cannot make me go out of my own accord. If you turn me out of your meetings I will stand on the outside,

and look in through the window, and see you.
If I cannot do this, I will come the next day and
sit in the place where you have been, and com-
mune with you so. I cannot be excommunicated,
for I shall continue thus always in your com-
munion.''

It was this quality of the Governor's mind
which prevented him always from identifying
himself with the sect of Abolitionists, who bore
the name of Mr. Garrison, although his opinions
on the subject of slavery were as decided as those
of their great leader, with whom he maintained a
friendship which continued unbroken to the close
of his life. The asperities of speech and indiscriminate denunciations which were frequent on
their platform also repelled him, and were dis-
pleasing to his kindly heart. He believed that
it was possible to hate slavery without hating
every slaveholder, and to abolish it without abolishing the Union; and he defined precisely his
position, in a letter written on July 31, 1860, in
reply to an invitation from Mr. Garrison to attend a meeting the next day to celebrate the
anniversary of British emancipation in the West
Indies.

"It is due,'' he wrote, '' to a perfectly frank
understanding, that I should say, what I believe
you already know, that though I am with you

and your friends in sympathy when you rejoice that the British slave is now a freeman, yet I have been so often pained at the unremitting and, I think, frequently unjust assaults by persons upon your platform on men whom I greatly respect, and whose services in the cause of rational and impartial liberty I highly prize, that I could not fail to esteem myself an intruder in your midst, unless I should suppress something I might feel urged to say.    My fidelity to the existing institution of government, its charters, its organization, and the duties of its citizenship, is, ever has been, and, I doubt not, will always be, unshaken ; but, working in the sphere of citizenship, and through the instrumentality it affords, I hope that I ever may remember the lesson of British emancipation, and apply it wherever I have the right and the power."

It has been mentioned that when in mature life he was called to be Governor, he was already a well-trained political philosopher.    Whether he would be as efficient in practice as he had been studious of theory was unknown.    The condition of his private fortune had debarred him from the practical political training which in this country almost always precedes elevation to the highest offices, and had required his uninterrupted devotion to a profession which always demands constancy as a condition of success. Never but once had he held political office, and then only for the session of 1859, as a member of the lower house of the Legislature, although, to be sure, he became the leader of that house, seizing the position in debate upon the question of an address for the removal of Edward G. Loring from the office of Judge of Probate for Suffolk County, which Mr. Loring held in violation of a statute of the Commonwealth rendering it incompatible with the office of United States' Commissioner, in which capacity Mr. Loring shortly before had acted in surrendering the fugitive slave Burns. At the close of the session he returned to his profession, declining an appointment to the bench of the Superior Court which was offered to him by Governor Banks, and refusing also to permit his name to be submitted to the convention of his party as a candidate for nomination for Governor. But, in 1860, notwithstanding this abstinence from official life, he was nominated for Governor by a genuine popular impulse which overwhelmed the old political managers, who regarded him as an intruder upon the arena, and had laid other plans.

His avowed sympathy with John Brown entered largely into the campaign; particularly an expression which he had used in taking the chair as presiding officer of a meeting for the relief of John Brown's family, on November 18, 1859, when (after reading to the audience a letter from Captain Brown to Lydia Maria Child telling what women and children would be left dependent on others by his death) he said : —

"I pause not now to consider, because it is wholly outside of the duty or the thought of this assembly to-night, whether the enterprise of John Brown and his associates in Virginia was wise or foolish, right or wrong; I only know that whether the enterprise itself was one or the other, *John Brown himself is right.* I sympathize with the man ; I sympathize with the idea ; because I sympathize with and believe in the Eternal Right. They who are dependent upon him and his sons and his associates in the battle at Harper's Ferry, have a right to call upon us who have professed to believe, or who have in any manner or measure taught the doctrine of the rights of man as applied to the colored slaves of the South, to stand by them in their bereavement, whether those husbands and fathers and brothers were right or wrong."

Timorous politicians from his own State and from others appealed to him in vain to retract, or at least to qualify these words. But he

would never take back or explain away one
syllable.

He had resolved, early in 1860, to devote himself to the national campaign, and in May was
Chairman of the Massachusetts delegation in
the Republican Convention at Chicago, where
after the final ballot, he was selected to second
the motion of Mr. Evarts that the nomination
of Mr. Lincoln for President should be made
unanimous. When in August he was himself
nominated for Governor, he did not throw up the
engagements he had made for speaking, but continued to canvass the State in person to the very
day of the election, when he was chosen by a
popular vote larger than had been received by
any of his predecessors.

In his inaugural address he recommended that
some considerable portion of the dormant militia
should be placed on a footing of activity, in order
that " in the possible contingencies of the future
the State might be ready without inconvenient
delay to contribute her share of force in any
exigency of public danger; " and he took a
broader and deeper view than was common in
those days of the magnitude of the impending
crisis, holding that in its issue was involved more
than the Union itself, — the very existence on
the face of the earth of democratic republi-

can government organized under constitutional forms.

"Upon this issue," he exclaimed, "over the heads of all mere politicians and partisans, in behalf of the Commonwealth of Massachusetts I appeal directly to the warm hearts and clear heads of the great masses of the people. The men who own and till the soil, who drive the mills, and hammer out their own iron and leather on their own anvils and lapstones, and they who, whether in the city or the country, reap the rewards of enterprising industry and skill in the varied pursuits of business, are honest, intelligent, patriotic, independent, and brave. They know that simple defeat in an election is no cause for the disruption of a government. They know that those who declare that they will not live peaceably within the Union do not mean to live peaceably out of it. They know that the people of all sections have a right which they mean to maintain, of free access from the interior to both oceans, and from Canada to the Gulf of Mexico, and of the free use of all the lakes and rivers and highways of commerce, North, South, East, or West. They know that the Union means Peace, and unfettered commercial intercourse from sea to sea and from shore to shore; that it secures us all against the unfriendly presence or possible dictation of any foreign power, and commands respect for our flag and security for our trade. And they do not intend, nor will they ever consent, to be excluded from these rights which they have so long enjoyed, or to abandon the prospect of the benefits which Humanity claims for itself by means of their continued enjoyment in the future."

## CHAPTER III.

Massachusetts Militia prepared for service. — Coöperation of other New England Governors invited. — Confidential understanding established with General Scott. — Troops held in readiness to be sent to Washington at counting of electoral vote for President. — The Governor's confidants at Washington. — The beginning of the War. — March of the Massachusetts Militia to Washington. — General review of the services of the Governor to the country during the war. — His counsel of sympathy with the Federal Government. — His unofficial advisers. — Vice President Hamlin summoned to Boston. — Union of all classes in Massachusetts in support of the war, under the Governor's leadership. — Mr. Evarts's description of his leadership. — Speech of Fletcher Webster on Bunker Hill. — Departure of the Twelfth Regiment.

THERE was a furious snow-storm on January 5, 1861, the day of his inauguration. Without waiting for it to abate, his first official act, immediately after the inaugural ceremonies, was to despatch a confidential messenger to the Governors of New Hampshire and Maine, to acquaint them with his determination to prepare the active militia of Massachusetts for instant service, and to invite their coöperation. Then followed, week by week, in the face of ridicule from many sources, and bitter opposition from many more, that series of military orders and those purchases of war material to which the whole country now looks back as evidences of unequaled foresight.

In the light of subsequent events his action in preparing Massachusetts for the war stands so fully justified that many have forgotten that it was opposed at all. But the records of the press and public assemblages and legislative proceedings during those trying weeks, bear witness that there was a large portion, even of the Governor's own political party, whose denunciation of it was exceeded only by their scoffing. Nothing, however, disturbed his steady purpose. The people to-day know how the troops were warned for duty by general orders issued in January, and soon afterwards contracts were made for the overcoats and other articles of equipment ; but they do not know yet the extent of his efforts, — how he urged that our militia should be summoned to garrison Washington at the time of the counting of the electoral votes for President and Vice President, in February ; how a confidential understanding was established between him and General Scott, which served more perhaps than any one other thing, to inspire the veteran commander with confidence that the country's cause was not hopeless ; how, in consultation with General Scott, written memoranda for the direction of our troops on the march to Washington were drawn up, by which it was provided, in anticipation of obstruction of their route overland, that they should proceed by sea and be disembarked either under cover of the guns of Fort McHenry at Baltimore, or else at Annapolis; and how steamers were kept for weeks in readiness at his bidding to transport them to the Chesapeake.

Besides General Scott, the persons at Washington who in those anxious days were intrusted with the Governor's confidence, were especially Charles Francis Adams and Montgomery Blair, and, to a certain extent, Edwin M. Stanton, who was then the Attorney General of President Buchanan. Referring to these offers of the Massachusetts troops, the latter, in a correspondence with ex-Governor Clifford (never yet published), wrote from Washington on February 11, 1861: "The determined and vigilant disposition to support the Government with requisite volunteer forces has produced here a beneficial effect and contributed to the anxiety of the revolutionists for concealing their designs."

At last the signal-gun of the Rebellion was fired. Patient in the extreme through all the attempts to prevent war, sympathizing and corresponding with Mr. Adams during all the efforts and proffers to the South which were made in the faint hope to avert it, yet when it came Governor Andrew welcomed it as the sure solution of all difficulties. In his own memorable words spoken in the address with which he opened the session of the General Court which was speedily called, " a grand era had dawned," and he " perceived nothing now about us which ought to discourage the good or to alarm the brave." " Senators and Representatives," said he, " grave responsibilities have fallen, in the providence of God, upon the government and people, — and they are welcome. They could not have been safely postponed. They have not arrived too soon. They will sift and try this people, all who lead and all who follow."

Never was a finer illustration of the couplet of the poet, that

" When once their slumbering passions burn,
The peaceful are the strong."

This man, of sympathies nurtured on the most advanced ideas of his age, yearning, hoping, praying for a peaceful end of all wrong, yet possessed a foresight so intuitive and a mind so practical, that he had calmly prepared for war, unmoved by the ridicule and abuse of men of coarser fibre ; and when war came, accepted it so solemnly and earnestly that there seemed and there was no inconsistency between his principle and his practice. "Devoted in heart to the interests of peace," said he in that same great address, "painfully alive to the calamities and sorrows of war, yet I cannot fail to see how plainly the rights and liberties of a people repose upon their own capacity to maintain them."

In an address delivered on June 17, 1865, on the occasion of dedicating the monument at Lowell to Ladd and Whitney, two of the men of the Sixth Massachusetts Regiment, who fell at Baltimore on the 19th of April, 1861, the Governor recurred to those early days of the war in words worthy of what he was describing : —

"It is not for me," he said, "to attempt to separate the bewildering masses of transactions and emotions through which we have lived, or to rise above the influence of those recent events which, at present, control alike the imagination and the reason. But I may testify to the impressions stamped forever on our memories and our hearts by that great week in April, when Massachusetts rose up at the sound of the cannonade of Sumter, and her militia brigade springing to their arms appeared on Boston Common. It redeemed the meanness and the weariness of many a prosaic life. It was a revelation of a profound sentiment, of manly faith, of glorious fidelity, and of a love stronger than death. Those were days of which none other in the history of the war became the parallel. And when, on the evening of the anniversary of the battle of Lexington, there came the news along the wires that the Sixth Regiment had been cutting its way through the streets of Baltimore, whose pavements were reddened with the blood of Middlesex, it seemed as if there descended into our hearts a mysterious strength and into our minds a supernal illumination. In many trying experiences of the war we have watched, by starlight as well as sunlight, the doubtful fortunes of our arms. But never has the news of victory, decisive and grand, — not even that of Gettysburg, on which hung issues more tremendous than ever depended on the fortunes of a single battle-field, — so lifted us above ourselves, so transformed our earthly weakness into heavenly might by a glorious transfiguration. The citizens of yesterday were to-day the heroes whom history would never forget ; and the fallen brave had put on the crown of martyrdom, more worthy than a hundred mortal diadems. Their blood alone was precious enough to wipe out the long arrears of shame. The great and necessary struggle was begun, without which we were a disgraced, a doomed, a ruined people. We had reached the parting of the ways ; and we had not hesitated

3

to choose the right one.    Oh! it is terrible, beyond expression terrible, to feel that only war, with all its griefs and pains and crimes, will save a people ; but how infinitely greater than the dread and the dismay with which we thought of war, was *the hope of that salvation !* ''

It is not within the province of this sketch to narrate the details of Governor Andrew's administration.    That duty is reserved for the biographer and the historian.    It is enough here to recall to memory how until after the Proclamation of Emancipation fixed the policy of the Federal Government, the war in behalf of the Union was rather a war of the States than of the Central Power ; and how, during the long and difficult interval, when every governor was a war-minister, he was the greatest of them all, clearest in foresight, most sagacious in counsel, most resolute in will, most untiring in action, undiscouraged himself by the faltering course of the Administration at Washington, lending it the aid of the financial credit of Massachusetts when its treasury was empty, raising and maintaining under arms troops for its service when it declared that it had " more men than were wanted," setting regiment after regiment in the field without calling on it for a single article of equipment, and, above all, encouraging it to appeal for its defense to the broad duty of allegiance owed by *all* its subjects.

Without the energy, patience, and determination of all the loyal governors, but especially of Governor Andrew in the East and Governor Morton of Indiana in the West, where to-day would have been the Union? The Central Government, its credit impaired, its arsenals empty, its fleets dispersed on remote seas, its counsels timorous and indecisive, was powerless alone to save it. Realizing all this, Governor Andrew, in his address to the Legislature on May 14, 1861, enjoined as the highest public duty the cultivation of a spirit of patience with the Federal Administration.

" In this grave national experience," he declared, " it becomes us not only to acquit ourselves as men, by courage and enterprise, but also to remember that every virtue, civil as well as military, calls on us with more commanding voice. Patient endurance, unflinching perseverance in every duty, whether of action or passion, at such a moment become grand and heroic. Nor can I urge too strongly the duty of faithful and filial union of heart with those to whom are committed the responsibilities of the central power. Whether they who have to guide the current of national action seem fast or slow, narrow or broad, I trust that Massachusetts men will, with equal devotedness, enact their part in this warfare as good soldiers of a great cause."

The men not holding official connection with his administration, whom chiefly he took into his confidence for counsel in these times, represented no one class of interests.    Among the merchants they were John M. Forbes and Francis B. Crowninshield; at the bar, Peleg W. Chandler and Horace Gray, jr.; from the bench, Judges Charles Allen and E. Rockwood Hoar; among men in political life, ex-Governor Boutwell * and Thomas D. Eliot.    Four of these, Judge Allen and ex-Governor Boutwell, and Messrs. Forbes and Crowninshield, he had appointed members of the " Peace Congress " which met at Washington in February at the request of the State of Virginia, and in which he completed the Massachusetts delegation of seven by adding Theoph-

* On consultation with ex-Governor Boutwell, on April 20, 1861, when communication was cut off between the North and Washington, and it was uncertain what might befall the President, Mr. Hamlin, the Vice President, was invited from his home in Maine to Boston by Governor Andrew, in order that if Washington, with the President, should fall into the hands of the rebels, the Federal Government might be immediately reorganized under the Vice President.    Upon the arrival of Mr. Hamlin at Boston a consultation took place between him and the Governor, and it was agreed that it would be best that any such organization, if necessary, should be effected at New York, whither he then proceeded.

ilus P. Chandler (the brother of Peleg W. Chandler), Richard P. Waters, and Mr. Goodrich, the Lieutenant Governor.

But the enthusiasm with which he inspired the people at a time when the hearty coöperation of all classes was essential to the honor of the State and the salvation of the Nation, was all his own. On the very first day of open hostilities, when it was seen how the preparations which he had been steadily pursuing in the face of ridicule and denunciation, were justified by the event, distrust vanished utterly. From that day forward, during his whole official term, he enjoyed the confidence of men of every class of society, pursuit in life, and shade of political opinion, to an extent more nearly universal than the history of the State records was ever reposed in another of its citizens ; and it was a confidence not conceded but commanded. The people recognized a natural leader. Mr. William M. Evarts has said truly : " Without adulation and without extravagance, we may say, looking at the actual career of Governor Andrew and at the public course of Massachusetts under his lead, that what Massachusetts did and what Massachusetts was during the years of our war, was a part of the fame of Governor Andrew, for he was the leading spirit, he was the preparing influence, his was the controlling mind, and his the unfailing energy, though it needed, of course, the great power and resources of the State for its manifestation." " And, besides his direct authority in his own State, who can measure the influence which he exerted over the colder natures or the duller intelligences of the public men of other States with whom he was brought in contact ? "

Men who had been political antagonists during a whole generation suspended, if they did not forget, their strife in answering his call. On the 17th of June, 1861, standing on Bunker Hill, he unfurled the flag of the Union on the monument (from the summit of which it was then for the first time displayed) ; and, standing by his side, the son of Daniel Webster spoke words which redeemed many an error of former years. " I renew," he said, " on this national altar vows not for the first time made, of devotion to my country, its Constitution and Union. I feel the inspiration which breathes around this spot. I feel the awful presence of the great dead who speak to us out of this hallowed ground. They call to us with more impressive than human voices to show ourselves not unworthy sons. From this spot I take my departure, like the mariner commencing his voyage, and wherever my eyes may close they will be turned hitherward — towards this NORTH." One month later Colonel Webster led his regiment from Massachusetts to Virginia, to fall on the field of Manassas on August 30, 1862; and as it marched down State Street in departing, the column joined in the chorus of

" John Brown's body lies a-mouldering in the grave,
But his soul is marching on ! "

No voice was raised that day to challenge the declaration that " John Brown himself was right."

## CHAPTER IV.

Arrangement and furniture of Executive rooms at the State House.
— Freedom of access of people to the Governor. — His catholic relation to all men. — Sir Frederick Bruce finds him surrounded by
colored people. — His habits of business. — Not an inch of red
tape. — His daily receptions. — His informal manner. — The
knapsack man. — Testimony of Mr. Hillard to the purity of his
life. — Testimony of Mr. Dana to his incorruptibility and humanity. — His power of endurance. — Neglect of private affairs. —
His love for children. — A visit to the White House at night. —
Rigid exaction of responsibility and work from others. — The
neglected pardon. — Care of penal institutions. — His relations
with the Executive Council.

THE arrangement of the private executive
rooms at the State House was unchanged during
the whole of the Governor's administration.    It
was faulty in many respects, and a few simple
changes in it, enabling him to seclude himself,
would have saved him from much care and an-
noyance.    They were on the same floor with
the Council Chamber, and were reached through
a long and narrow corridor which led into an
antechamber.    Out of this the Governor's apartment opened directly, with no intervening room.
It was a low-studded chamber, perhaps twenty-
five feet square, lighted by two windows opening

westward. In the centre was a massive square table, on the side of which, facing the door of the antechamber, the Governor had his seat. Directly opposite him, at the same table, sat his secretary. At a desk near one of the windows was the place of an assistant secretary. The chairs and sofa were very plain and covered with green plush. The large book-cases along the northern wall, empty at the beginning of his administration, became filled before the end of it with more than two hundred volumes of the correspondence conducted under his immediate direction. A large mirror, with a heavily carved black-walnut frame, surmounted the mantel, gas-fixtures projecting from among the carving; and on these, during the first year of the war, while Massachusetts was arming and equipping her own troops, he was accustomed to hang specimens of shoddy clothing or defective accoutrements, labelled with the names of the faithless contractors, thus publicly exposed to the indignation of the hundreds of visitors who frequented the room. His only means of seclusion was to retreat into a room beyond the antechamber, from which there was no other outlet than the door of entrance, which was of solid iron. Every frequenter of the State House may remember seeing him, after being pestered beyond endurance, hasten across the antechamber into this room, where he would bolt and bar out the waiting crowd until he could finish some urgent work demanding freedom from the interruptions to which he was subject in his own apartment.  Once behind that iron door he was free ; and it was the only place in the whole building where he was secure from intrusion.

His patience, however, under all manners of interruption, was marvelous.  Now and then it would give way in little acts of nervousness, such as pulling unconsciously at a bell-rope which hung over his table, or insisting on the immediate attendance of an old and favorite clerk from the Adjutant-General's office who had been dead a year or more.  By some curious psychological process, when the Governor had been especially vexed at anything which went wrong in that office, he more than once forgot the old gentleman's death, and sent down stairs for him.

He was accessible always to all kinds and conditions of people, and in the freedom of his intercourse with them he fully exemplified and might well have adopted the words with which De Quincey, in his " Confessions," introduces the story of the friendless girl of the London streets :

" The truth is, that at no time of my life have I been a person to hold myself polluted by the touch or approach of any person who wore a

human shape ; on the contrary, from my very
earliest youth, it has been my pride to converse
freely, *more Socratico*, with all human beings,
man, woman, and child, that chance might fling
in my way, — a practice which is friendly to the
knowledge of human nature, to good feelings,
and to that frankness of address which becomes
a man who would be thought a philosopher, for
a philosopher should not see with the eyes of the
poor limitary creature calling himself a man of
the world and filled with narrow and self-regard-
ing prejudices of birth and education, but should
look upon himself as a catholic creature, and as
standing in an equal relation to high and low, to
educated and uneducated, to the guilty and innocent."

Countless anecdotes might be repeated illustrating this trait of his character, but there is
room here only for one, which was aptly told by
Mr. Edwin P. Whipple in his eulogy before the
city government of Boston : —

" Sir Frederick Bruce, the British Minister,
once called upon the Governor at the State
House and found the room nearly filled with colored women who had come to him to obtain news
of fathers, brothers and sons enlisted in the black
regiments of Massachusetts. Sir Frederick
waited, while the Governor, with kindly patience,

listened to complaints, answered questions, gave advice, and tried to infuse consolation and cheer into the hearts of his humble friends. After these interviews were all over the turn of the British minister came, and he was a man with the nobility of soul to appreciate what he had witnessed. Clasping the Governor by the hand, he declared that, whatever might be the advantages of a republican government, he had never believed that it could assume a paternal character, but what he had just seen proved how much he had been mistaken."

His habits of business lacked system, in part through inexperience of official life, but more through eagerness to dispose at once of the matters uppermost. He never acquiesced patiently in any routine. Writing to President Lincoln on May 3, 1861, he said: "On receiving your proclamation [calling for troops] we took up the war and have carried on our part of it in the spirit in which, we believe, the Administration and the American people intend to act; namely, as if there was not an inch of red tape in the world."

So far, however, as he may be said to have had a daily routine, it was his custom to devote the early hours of the morning, first to his mail; then to reports from the departments of the State

government, and interviews with officials of those
departments and with officers of the United
States having business with him ; then to interviews with officers from the field or engaged in
recruiting or organizing troops at home ; and
finally, at some time between noon and one
o'clock, to throw open the doors of his room to
the public. By that hour a great crowd had
assembled in the antechamber, eager for admit-
tance. Except the similar though rarer public
receptions by President Lincoln, there were no
scenes in which it was possible to witness more
of the effect of the war on all classes of society
than in those daily inroads. Instantly the room
would be filled with the crowd. Then, with that
patience which almost never failed, he would
hear and examine personally into every case, or
give the applicant in charge to his staff-officers
to make the examination under his own supervision, and would do all that could be done to
relieve suffering or anxiety, stimulate patriotism
or reward merit.

He had not that smooth way of refusing without seeming to refuse, in which his predecessor
so excelled. It was often to be wished, for his
own comfort, that he could develop ever so small
a degree of that official manner which checks
and repels intrusion ; but he never did. There

was not, in his nature, the germ of formalism. One day, among the many exhibitors of military notions who beset him, was a man with a patent knapsack. There were many visitors in attendance, some of high distinction, awaiting audience; but the knapsack man was before them in obtaining his ear. He listened to his description of the article; and when he was told that some of our Massachusetts troops wished it as a substitute for the regulation knapsack, he forgot the presence of everybody, asked for it to be packed and buckled over his own shoulders, and then marched up and down the room, testing himself its asserted merits, before he would turn to any other business.

In those daily receptions, women anxious for the safety or health of fathers, sons, brothers, husbands, in the armies before Richmond or Vicksburg, or in the rebel prisons, or having grievances to present as to the administration of " State aid " to their families; soldiers complaining of injustice or of suffering in the field or at home; selectmen and recruiting committees suggesting plans or asking favors to promote enlistments; an endless host of applicants for appointments, military and civil; citizens of every class seeking indorsement and aid of schemes for sanitary and other charities; petitioners for pardon of criminals, for admission of deaf and dumb or blind or idiotic children as public beneficiaries to the charitable institutions of the State, — these, and a countless multitude of others, on every conceivable variety of business, all found a willing ear and an attention justly proportioned to their affairs, whether serious or trivial. To all these various wants and needs never was a heart more sensitive, never a disposition more paternal ; and this recalls the testimony borne by Mr. George S. Hillard, his political opponent, but his life-long friend, when (at the same bar meeting at which Mr. Chandler gave the description of the Governor's college life, already quoted), after first declaring his belief that the loss of Governor Andrew was a greater loss to Massachusetts than that of any citizen either in the early or the later history of the State, he said that, " in conclusion, he wished to make another remark, which might seem as extraordinary as that with which he opened his address, but which he believed sincerely was truth ; and that was that he never knew a man whose daily life and conversation embodied the teachings of the Saviour as laid down in Holy Writ more than his. He never knew a man who left this world with less of the stain of sin than he."

And Mr. Richard H. Dana Jr., who preceded

Mr. Hillard on the same occasion, after styling Governor Andrew " a great magistrate and an incorruptible man," continued, —

" I do not say incorruptible in that low and mean sense of being above pecuniary temptation : I should feel it derogatory to him even to allude to such an exemption ; although, as times go, there are cases in which it is no small praise.   I mean to say that he could not be deflected from the course of duty by any of the temptations which address themselves to the weaknesses of public men.   His morality was not a graft of later years upon an ordinary stock ; it was not sweet water gathered into a vase, nor the accumulations of a large reservoir ; but it was a fountain of living water, springing up from the depths of his nature.   The foundations of his character were laid deep and strong.

" In the older civilizations and religions there were scattered instances of humane men who recognized more or less the obligations or the claims of man, as such, upon his fellow-men ; but they ended as they began, with closet reflections or sublime sentiments for the reading of the few ; there never was a religion until Christianity, that even professed a recognition of the great truth to which Christianity commands the obedience of all ; that is, the truth of the unity of mankind, the substantial equality in kind of every human being, children of one Maker, who will not allow the weakest and the meanest of them to be neglected. Mr. Andrew felt to the utmost this Christian obligation, and fulfilled it with enthusiasm. No cry struck his ear in which he could recognize even the articulate sound which is the proof of humanity, that he did not listen to. Let a cry for justice come even from the debased or the wicked, he was ready to examine, and if right to assert. A plea for a right, though it came from those who had all their lives done nothing but wrong, had its distinct claim upon him as a citizen and a man. His sympathies were quick and sincere, but it is no uncommon thing for mere sensibility to weep over pain and distress, and even to relieve it ; this he would do, but his large mind and thoughtful habits led him to address himself to the causes of vice, and suffering, and wrong. He was not satisfied with relieving the sufferer or the oppressed ; he addressed himself to attack the causes of oppression and suffering.

" I have used the word incorruptible in its highest sense, but we have not exhausted it. He appreciated office and station as opportunities for the exercise of powers which he felt that he possessed for the good of mankind, and he loved to

4

be in the march of great events, as an incitement
to virtuous activity. But he would not accept
any post for the exercise of power, whatever its
opportunities for doing good, upon any terms
whatever that might restrict or qualify his moral
power. He had absolute faith in the moral government of a Supreme Being, for whose power
nothing was too great, and for whose supervision
nothing was too minute. He knew that however
a man may be helmed and shielded and harnessed
by skill and art, there was always a spear of truth
which could pierce through the joints of the har-
ness, and inflict a wound past all surgery. He
felt that he could not exercise his intellectual
powers except in a clear moral atmosphere; and
in such an atmosphere, though he was neither
vain nor rash, he was ready, aye, ready for the
encounter; for he had absolute faith. Whatever
might be the appearance of weakness around
him, and however slight might be his visible
support, he knew that the very winds blew and
waters rolled strength to the brave, and power
and victory."

In spite of the harassing character of cares like
those which have been described, on a nature so
sympathetic as was that of Governor Andrew,
his power of endurance was extraordinary. Almost invariably he was at the State House as

early or even earlier than either of his secretaries, and his appearance was always the signal for fresh work in every department of the building. Paying hasty calls at the offices of the Adjutant-General and the Surgeon-General, on his way, nine o'clock rarely found him absent from his own desk ; and there he continued always until sunset, and often until long past midnight, unless some public duty called him elsewhere.

His private affairs went utterly neglected. His family he rarely saw by daylight, except in the early morning and on Sundays, and to a man of so affectionate a disposition this was the greatest sacrifice. Even on Sundays there was often no respite of work. Sometimes, however, his children would come to his crowded room at the State House, and linger there for an hour in the early afternoon on their way home from school. No matter how urgent his business, there was always a moment to spare for an affectionate word or a caress, and an encouragement to make a play-room of the chamber.

James Freeman Clarke relates a characteristic anecdote which belongs in this connection. He says : " A pleasant picture comes up in my mind of an evening in Washington at the end of 1861. Brother Andrew took me with him to the White House to see President Lincoln. It

was about ten o'clock, but the porter said that
the President had gone out with Mr. Seward;
but, recognizing Governor Andrew, he added,
'Walk in, Governor, walk in.'    So Brother
Andrew went in, and looked through all the
rooms of the lower floor.    All were lighted, and
all empty.    Then he went up-stairs, and I followed.    We came to a door before which stood
two pairs of little shoes.    'This is the children's
room,' said he; 'I should like to go in and see
them asleep.'    He put his hand on the handle
of the door, as if to open it, and then, changing
his mind, turned away.    But the impulse was
such a natural one!    In the palace of the nation,
in the midst of the great rebellion, the image of
these little children quietly asleep took his heart
for the moment away from all the great affairs
of the State and Nation."

During the first few months of the war his
labor at the State House averaged more than
twelve hours daily, and during April and May,
1861, the gray light of morning often mingled
with the gaslight over his table, before he abandoned work, discharged his weary attendants,
and walked down the hill to his little house in
Charles Street to snatch a few hours of sleep before beginning the task of another day.    It must
have been an iron constitution as well as an iron

will which sustained these irregularities with constantly renewing vigor. After his invariable bath and hasty breakfast he would reappear at the State House as fresh as the morning itself, without a trace perceptible to the casual visitor of irritation or fatigue, while perhaps half an hour later his attendants of the previous night would come to their places cross and jaded. Mr. Clarke says well: " He worked like the great engine in the heart of the steamship. The vessel may be rolling and pitching amidst frightful seas, her decks swept by successive waves, but there, in the centre of the ship, the engine works steadily on with tranquil accuracy but enormous power. Such force, so steadily exercised, was his. There was no jar, no strain, no hurry, no repose ; but constant equable motion, on and on, through all those weary years, to their triumphant end."

Unsparing to himself, he did not spare others ; filled himself with a sustaining enthusiasm, he expected and demanded from others efforts corresponding in proportion to their ability. His secretary once recommended to him an increase of the pay of a subordinate. The letter bears the indorsement instantly made : " I cordially assent, but *on condition* that he shall come at nine o'clock, A. M." This was in the case of an officer whose residence was out of the city, and whose duties kept him at the State House almost always until sunset and often until midnight. It was an indorsement not unkind, — never from all those years can any of his associates or subordinates recall a single act or word of unkindness done or spoken by Governor Andrew, — but it was characteristic of his habit to hold every one strictly to the full measure of duty. So was his indignation, one dreary afternoon, the day before Christmas, at finding that the office of the Secretary of the Commonwealth was closed half an hour earlier than usual. There was a severe snow-storm raging, which suspended business through the city, and the clerks of that office had closed it, forgetting that there should have been drawn and forwarded up-stairs during the day, for the Governor's signature, a pardon which had been granted to a convict in the State Prison, according to a custom which prevailed with him to grant one pardon, upon the recommendation of the Warden, every Christmas morning. It irritated him that the clerks below should have forgotten such a duty. During his own hard work through the day, the thought of the happiness which the morrow would bring to that convict had lightened his heart, and he felt a positive pain that others should not have shared that feeling. Though unwell, he hastily broke out of the room, walked through the driving snow across the city to the house of one of the officers of the State Department, brought him back to the State House, stood by him while the pardon was drawn and the Great Seal of the Commonwealth was affixed to it, signed it, and then despatched it by one of his secretaries to the Warden at Charlestown.

The preliminary investigation of applications for pardon he seldom delegated to others, even at the height of his military labor. By the Constitution of the State, the assent of the Council was necessary to confirm every pardon proposed by the Governor, and there was a regular committee for formal investigation of pardon cases ; but he did not often decide to refer any particular application to that committee, until after some preliminary investigation himself, frequently involving no little toil. During his term of office there was hardly a place of confinement of criminals in the whole Commonwealth, from Nantucket to Berkshire, which he did not personally visit. He believed that care of our penal institutions was next in importance for the welfare of the State, to the care of the schools.

The legal obligation to consult the Council, not only with regard to all matters of pardon, but with regard also to almost all matters whatsoever of administration, whether of finance or appointment, was a great drain upon his patience. But there were certain advantages in it which he was quick to appreciate. Chiefly, it methodized in his own mind the reasons for his acts. The necessity oftentimes of expressing reasons to the Council, and the liability at all times to be called on to express them, compelled him to avoid altogether that vagueness of thought which accompanies the actions of most men. Almost daily, during the war, there was a session of the Council at which he was obliged to attend for one, two, or three hours. Usually it began in the early afternoon, after the close of his public reception.

# CHAPTER V.

The Governor's habits of diet. — Liking of tea. — His opposition to a Prohibitory Liquor Law. — Extracts from his argument. — He abstains from presenting the subject to the Legislature while Governor, lest he should divide the people from support of the war. — His message to the Legislature on the morality of sale of liquors as a beverage. — Union in sustaining the War paramount to all other issues. — He combats Western hostility to New England. — His theory of the destiny of New England in event of success of the Rebellion. — His views of the relations of the British Provinces to New England.

BEFORE leaving his own apartment for the Council Chamber the Governor was accustomed to retreat from visitors into a little intermediate room, where he partook of a simple lunch, generally of only bread and cheese with a cup of tea. Dr. Johnson was not a more devoted lover of tea. He held to the theory that it is a positive nourisher of nervous force, and always was ready to drink it at any time of day or night.

Simple in all his diet, although, like almost all busy professional men, a hearty and rapid eater, he enjoyed and appreciated the pleasures of the table, for he was a ·thoroughly developed man in all the elements of manhood, physical as well as intellectual and moral. In his great argument against the principle of a prohibitory liquor law, made in the winter of 1867 before a committee of the Legislature, while reciting the causes which combined to increase the perils of New Englanders from drunkenness, besides "a hard climate, much exposure, few amusements, a sense of care and responsibility cultivated intensely, and the prevalence of ascetic and gloomy theories of life, duty, and Providence," he enumerates also " the absence of light, cheering beverages, little variety in food, and great want of culinary skill." He was fond of wine and used it freely, but always with temperance ; and he despised, from the bottom of his heart, the prevailing hypocrisy as to its use. No one respected more the discretion of the individual who should abstain from it, either for fear of being tempted beyond self-control, or for example to others in danger ; but he demanded equal respect for his own discretion.

Believing that law has of itself no reforming power, that it may punish and terrify but cannot convert, he attacked the doctrine of prohibitory legislation at its root.

" It is," he argued, " only in the strife and actual controversy of life — natural, human, and free — that robust virtue can be attained, or positive good accomplished. It is only in similar freedom alike from bondage and pupilage, alike from the prohibitions of artificial legislation on the one hand, and superstitious fears on the other, that nations or peoples can become thrifty, happy, and great. Will you venture to adhere to the effete blunders of antiquated despotisms, in the hope of serving, by legal force, the moral welfare of your posterity? Will you insist on the dogma that, even if certain gifts of nature or science are not poisons, they are nevertheless so dangerously seductive that no virtue can be trusted to resist them? But when society shall have intrusted the keeping of its virtue to the criminal laws, who will guaranty *your* success in the experiment, tried by so many nations and ages, resulting always in failure and defeat? Do you exclaim, that the permitted sale of these beverages, followed as it must be by some use, must be followed, in turn, by some drunkenness; and that drunkenness is not only the parent cause of nearly all our social woes, but that it is impossible to maintain against its ravages a successful moral war? To both these propositions, moral philosophy, human experience, and history, all command a respectful dissent.

" Reason, experience, and history all unite to prove that, while drunkenness lies in near relations with poverty and other miseries, and is very often their proximate cause, it is not true that it is the parent, or essential cause, without which they would not have been. And to the teachings of reason, experience, and history, are added the promises of Gospel Grace, enabling me in all boldness to confront the fears of those who would rest the hopes of humanity on the commandments of men."

" Drunkenness was naturally one of the forms which vice assumed in New England. So far as it depended on the mere fact of opportunity for indulgence, it was partly due to our nearness to the West Indies, and to the trade by which our lumber was exchanged for their molasses. The peculiar product of our distillation was the result of the lumber trade with the West India Islands, just as the production of whiskey is now the result of the superabundant grain crops of the Western States. A hard climate, much exposure, little variety in food, and great want of culinary skill, few amusements, the absence of light, cheering beverages, a sense of care and responsibility cultivated intensely, and the prevalence of ascetic and gloomy theories of life, duty, and Providence — have, in time past, all combined to increase the perils of the people from the seductive narcotic. A man whose virtue was weak, or whose discouragements were great, or whose burdens were heavy, or in whom the spirit waged unequal war with the allurements of the flesh; or even one in whom a certain native gayety strove with the unwelcome exactions of the elders, was often easily its victim. Independence, intelligence, self-respect, broader views, kinder and tenderer sympathies, the cultivation of the finer tastes, the love and appreciation of beauty, a truer humanity, — not to speak of better social theories, — all made more general and pervading in our society, have gradually, by divine favor, been made instrumental in the deliverance of our people from that bondage. I have not mentioned *a greater conscientiousness* in the catalogue of causes, for I do not believe that conscientiousness has ever been greater than in New England, or that it is greater now than it was in other times. It was a characteristic of New England from the first. It was always a source of greatness in her people. But it has been often morbid and even superstitious.

" The evil of drunkenness needed to be met by a gracious Gospel kindling the heart, not by a crushing sense of guilt goading the conscience. The temperance reformation sprang up out of the heart of a deeply moved humanity. It was truly and genuinely a Gospel work. It was a mission of love and hope.    And the power with which it wrought was the evidence of its inspiration.    While it held fast by its original simplicity, while it pleaded, with the self-forgetfulness of Gospel discipleship, and sought out with the generosity of an all-embracing charity, while it twined itself around the heart-strings and quietly persuaded the erring, or with an honest boldness rebuked without anger, — it was strong in the Lord and in the power of his might, verifying the prophecy of old, that one might chase a thousand and two put ten thousand to flight. But when it passed out of the hands of its Evangelists and passed into the hands of the centurions and the hirelings ; when it became a part of the capital of political speculation, and went into the jugglery of the caucus ; when men voted to lay abstinence as a burden on their neighbors, while they felt no duty of such abstinence themselves (even under the laws of their own creation) ; when the Gospel, the Christian Church, and the ministers of religion were yoked to the car of a political triumph ; then it became the victim of one of the most ancient and most dangerous of all the delusions of history."

In all his life, public and private, there was not a single act which afforded him more internal satisfaction than this attack.    The subject had been with him one of earnest thought and clear conviction for many years; but for fear of dividing the people on a local question when they should be united on the great national issues, he abstained from presenting it to the Legislature until after the war. The result of the State election that occurred the week after his death, completely revolutionizing the policy of Massachusetts on the question, and vindicating his position, was a proof of the sagacity with which he foresaw the verdict of the people on a theory of legislation which only one year before it required high moral courage even to challenge; and the planless action of the Legislature which the revolution brought into power, has proved also how dependent it was upon his leadership for a successful conclusion.

Once only, while he was Governor, did the Legislature force him to an official intimation of the opinions which he was so well known to entertain, by passing and presenting for his signature, in 1865, a resolve "that it is not expedient or right in principle to authorize the sale of intoxicating liquors as a beverage, by license." It was notorious that the purpose of many who were concerned in the passage of this resolve, was to embarrass him. As usual, the straightforward simplicity with which he met every issue, disap-

pointed their shallow calculations. Inquiry having been made in the Senate as to the Governor's
action upon this resolve, he quietly sent to that
branch of the Legislature a message saying: —

"Since the inquiry has been mooted, I deem it
not only appropriate, but more respectful to the
General Court that I should communicate for its
information the views entertained by me and
which direct my action in the premises. On reading the resolve, it is apparent that the signature
of the Governor would not give to it the force
of law, or change its character, significance, or
value, since the resolve is only the expression of
an opinion on an abstract proposition. Were I
to add my official approval I should be guilty of
the affectation of presuming to the right of ap-
proving or disapproving the opinions on questions
of morality and ethics entertained by gentlemen
whose opinions are, I presume, at least as valuable as my own, and which my mere approval or
disapproval could not affect. There are resolves,
such as those which presume to utter the opinions
of the people, our common constituency, on public affairs ; or to express their gratitude to public
servants for distinguished merit and exertions for
the common good ; or their condolence with those
who share with all the people the grief of a common public calamity [referring to the then recent

death of President Lincoln] ; in which resolves it seems proper for the Governor to unite officially, since he also is a representative of the Commonwealth. But it does not seem to me that with becoming regard to the entire independence with which opinions should be entertained, he can affect to revise the opinions expressed in a resolve such as the one above recited."

During the war, his determination to unite Massachusetts in its support was paramount to every other consideration, and was the key to many acts which pained some of his friends and offended others. The deference to certain classes of society of which he was accused in some of his appointments, was only one feature of a settled policy. Many a gallant young officer went down from Massachusetts into Virginia to battle, an unconscious hostage for the loyalty of men at home who in times of disaster might otherwise easily have fallen into indifference or opposition. This deep determination was rewarded with success. Massachusetts was a unit from the day when the flag ceased to fly over Sumter to the day when it crowned again the ruins of the fort. Divided, we might have perished. United, we led the van of the war. No one felt the perils of discord more than he, especially during that period when there was talk of " leaving New

England out in the cold." The official records of those days show how he pleaded and argued with the West for a more cordial union; * but while he had an implicit trust in the issue of the war as it did result, yet he had too little pride of opinion, and was too truly a statesman, not to consider and provide against a different issue. In event of the success of the Rebellion, he anticipated the formation of a northeastern confederacy which should combine the greater part of New England with Nova Scotia, New Brunswick, and a part of Canada ; and if our present Union had been doomed to failure, he would not have considered such a destiny for Massachusetts as hopeless. In such a confederacy he beheld all the elements of a first-rate power, — a homogeneous population of more than five millions, rapidly increasing ; the great harbors of Boston, Portland, and Halifax, with a capacity to command the commerce of the Northern Atlantic ; control of the outlet of the great lakes by possession of the southern bank of the St. Lawrence ; mines of iron and coal ; forests of timber for every use of architecture and navigation ; the mechanic arts

---

* See particularly his printed letter to S. F. Wetmore of Indiana, February 3, 1863, in reference to the relative contributions of Massachusetts and Indiana for the war, and to the contributions of Massachusetts for the development of the Northwest; and his inaugural address to the Legislature of 1864.

fully developed ; manufactures in maturity ; and education, literature, and the fine arts at the highest point of culture they have attained in America. But his heart was with the Union as it is. Never in public letter or speech did he tolerate the idea of its failure. He had an abiding faith in God's will to preserve it ; and with him faith always availed more than reason, the heart more than the intellect. But intellectually regarding the success of the Rebellion as a possibility, he devoted much attention to the relations of the British Provinces to New England, a study to which he was previously attracted, also, by a conviction that in more intimate bonds of commerce with them Boston would find rich sources of material prosperity. After retiring from office his interest in the subject even increased. He was deeply concerned for the success of the railway by which uninterrupted communication will be effected between Boston and Halifax ; and during the summer before his death he passed his vacation in a tour through the Provinces.

## CHAPTER VI.

His antagonism with opponents of emancipation and the use of
colored troops. — Support of Frémont and Hunter in freeing
slaves. — Letter in defense of Hunter. — Speech at Martha's
Vineyard. — His influence on the President for Emancipation. —
The Proclamation of September 22, 1862. — The Altoona Convention. — Address of the Governors to the President. — His independence of partisan influences and considerations. — Opposition to secret societies. — Jealousy towards him of old party
leaders. — His vetoes. — Official appointments and removals, civil
and military. — The duty of allegiance the solution of the problem
of emancipation. — Correspondence with General McClellan concerning exclusion of fugitive slaves from our military lines. —
Correspondence with General Butler concerning proper relations
of our military forces to servile insurrection in Maryland in
April, 1861.

MUCH has been said, since his death, of his
unvarying sweetness of disposition, which is liable
to give a wrong impression of the man. In a
memoir which he prepared in 1860 of a friend
with whom, he wrote, he had sustained " an in-
timacy of acquaintance such as never existed
between himself and any other man," and whose
influence on his character was continuous for
fourteen years,* he described one quality of his

* The late John W. Browne, of Hingham.

friend's nature in language which may well be applied to his own, saying, " He was terribly bold when truth demanded. And his courage began at home. He always accused and tried himself before he denounced any other man. Hence flowed a sense of freedom, — a self-emancipation, — which liberated him from the thousand bonds which hamper men who are constrained by the necessities of pretense and sham. This also cleared his mental vision and his perception of moral distinctions, so that he walked in the green pastures and beside the still waters of a life obedient to the precepts of a sincere heart and a transparent intellect." So Governor Andrew never allowed himself to be drawn into a quarrel, and had no personal hatred, even against those who did him most grievous personal wrong. But his whole soul was devoted to the grand principles of civil and political liberty which were at stake in the war ; and with some men who, he believed, were obstructing right and justice in the policy of the government he was in mortal antagonism. Such hatreds as those he cherished intensely, and they harmonized with his natural kindness like shade and light in a fine painting. No one could be familiar with the steps toward emancipation, and the use of colored troops, without being sensible of his strong antipathies to certain men who obstructed those measures.

Over the bodies of our soldiers who were killed at Baltimore he had recorded a prayer that he might live to see the end of the war, and a vow that, so long as he should govern Massachusetts, and so far as Massachusetts could control the issue, it should not end without freeing every slave in America.  He believed, at the first, in the policy of emancipation as a war measure. Finding that timid counsels controlled the government at Washington, and the then commander of the Army of the Potomac, so that there was no light in that quarter, he hailed the action of Frémont in Missouri in proclaiming freedom to the western slaves.  Through all the reverses which afterwards befell that officer he never varied from this friendship ; and when at last Frémont retired from the Army of Virginia, the Governor offered him the command of a Massachusetts regiment, and vainly urged him to take the field again under our State flag.  Just so, afterwards, he welcomed the similar action of Hunter in South Carolina, and wrote in his defense the famous letter in which he urged "to fire at the enemy's magazine." *  He was deeply

* Premising that this letter, dated May 19, 1862, was written in reply to a request of the Secretary of War to be advised within what

disappointed when the Administration disavowed Hunter's act, for he had hoped much from the personal friendship which was known to exist between the General and the President. Soon followed the great reverses of McClellan before Richmond.

The feelings of the Governor at this time on the subject of emancipation are well expressed in a speech which he made on August 10, 1862, at the Methodist camp-meeting on Martha's Vineyard. It was the same speech in which occurs his remark, since so often quoted : —

" I know not what record of sin awaits me in

---

limit of time Massachusetts could furnish a certain number of additional regiments, if the Federal Government should call for them, the passages in it which were especially denounced by those who at that time opposed the use of colored soldiers and the project of emancipation, were as follows : —

" If our people feel that they are going into the South to help fight rebels who will kill and destroy *them* by all the means known to savages as well as civilized man ; will deceive them by fraudulent flags of truce and lying pretenses (as they did the Massachusetts boys at Williamsburg); will use their negro slaves against them both as laborers and as fighting men, while they themselves must never fire at the enemy's magazine, I think they will feel that the draft is heavy on their patriotism. But, if the President will sustain General Hunter, recognize *all* men, even black men, as legally capable of that loyalty the blacks are waiting to manifest, and let them fight with God and human nature on their side, the roads will swarm, if need be, with multitudes whom New England would pour out to obey your call. Always ready to do my utmost, I remain most faithfully," etc.

the other world, but this I know, that I was never mean enough to despise any man because he was ignorant, or because he was poor, or because he was black."

Referring to slavery, he said : —

" I have never believed it to be possible that this controversy should end, and Peace resume her sway, until that dreadful iniquity has been trodden beneath our feet. I believe it cannot, and I have noticed, my friends (although I am not superstitious, I believe), that, from the day our government turned its back on the proclamation of General Hunter, the blessing of God has been withdrawn from our arms. We were marching on, conquering and to conquer ; post after post had fallen before our victorious arms ; but since that day I have seen no such victories. But I have seen no discouragement. I bate not one jot of hope. I believe that God rules above, and that he will rule in the hearts of men, and that, either with our aid or against it, he has determined to let the people go. But the confidence I have in my own mind that *the appointed hour has nearly come,* makes me feel all the more confidence in the certain and final triumph of our Union arms, because I do not believe that this great investment of Providence is to be wasted."

The allusion to the impending Proclamation of Emancipation by the President will be observed. Daily now for two years the Governor had not ceased to labor for it, in public and private. By speech and letter and personal appeal, by every appliance which wisdom and ingenuity could suggest, he had helped to work on the President for that end. But up to the final moment he trembled lest Mr. Lincoln might not be equal to the emergency. He knew that General McClellan had written to the President from Harrison's Landing, that " a declaration of radical views, especially upon slavery, will rapidly disintegrate our present armies ; " and it was to strengthen the purpose of the President that he joined at this time in the project of the convention of Governors at Altoona. His intention was to counteract the influence of McClellan and the " conservatives," by uniting the various States, through their chief magistrates, in an expression of loyalty and a pledge of support to the President in declaring emancipation as a military necessity. The plan had effect. The Governors were on their way to Altoona when the President anticipated their purpose, and preferred to accept their support of an act already done rather than their counsel to do it. Governor Andrew was at Philadelphia when the

Proclamation of September 22 appeared. He sent back to Boston that day an unofficial letter too characteristic to be omitted.

" PHILADELPHIA, *September* 22, 1862.

"DEAR A——: Before starting for Altoona, I have telegraphed to Mr. Claflin, and I now write more fully to you. The Proclamation of Emancipation by the President is out. It is a poor *document*, but a mighty *act ;* slow, somewhat halting, wrong in its delay till January, but grand and sublime after all. 'Prophets and kings' have waited for this day, but died without the sight. *We* must take up the silver trumpet and repeat the immortal strain on every hill-top and in every household of New England. Our Republicans must make it *their* business to sustain this act of Lincoln, and we will drive the 'conservatism' of a pro-slavery Hunkerism and the reactionaries of despotism into the very caves and holes of the earth. The conquest of the rebels, the emancipation of the slaves, and the restoration of peace founded on liberty and permanent democratic ideas ! Let this be our platform. No bickerings, no verbal criticism, no doubting Thomases, must halt the conquering march of triumphant liberty. Go IN FOR THE WAR. Hurry up the recruitments. Have grand *war meetings* all over the State. I hope our friends will begin at Faneuil Hall to-morrow night. Let not the rebels gain by delays, either in Massachusetts or in the field. We can ' knock the bottom out ' of the Hunker ' citizens' ' movement before ten days are gone. But tell Claflin, Sumner, Wilson, etc., etc., to *strike quick. Now*, now, NOW ! Our cause is bright if we are true.

Yours ever,

JOHN A. ANDREW."

The address to the President in which the Governors united on September 24 at Altoona, was written by Governor Andrew. Those passages which relate to the Proclamation of Emancipation were as follows : —

" We hail with heartfelt gratitude and encouraged hope the Proclamation of the President issued on the 22d of September, declaring emancipated from their bondage all persons held to service or labor as slaves in the rebel States where rebellion shall last until the 1st day of January now next ensuing. The right of any persons to retain authority to compel any portion of the subjects of the National Government to rebel against it or to maintain its enemies, implies in those who are allowed possession of such authority, the right to rebel themselves. And therefore the right to establish martial law or military government in a State or Territory in rebellion implies the right and the duty of such government to liberate the minds of all men living therein, by appropriate proclamations and assurances of protection, in order that all who are capable, intellectually and morally, of loyalty and obedience, may not be forced into treason and become unwilling tools of rebellious traitors. To have continued indefinitely the most efficient cause, support, and stay of the rebellion would have been, in our judgment, unjust to the loyal people whose treasure and lives are made a willing sacrifice on the altar of patriotism; would have discriminated against the wife who is compelled to surrender her husband, and against the parent who surrenders his child to the hardships of the camp and the perils of battle, in favor of rebel masters permitted to retain their slaves. It would have been a final decision alike against humanity, against the right and duty of the government, and against sound and wise national policy.    The decision of the President to strike at the root of the rebellion will lend new vigor to the efforts and new life and hope to the hearts of the people.

" Cordially tendering to the President our respectful assurances of personal and official confidence, we trust and believe that the policy now inaugurated will be crowned with success, will give speedy and triumphant victory over our enemies, and secure to this Nation and this People the blessing and favor of Almighty God. We believe that the blood of the heroes who have already fallen, and of those who may yet give their lives to their country, will not have been shed in vain."

The coincidence of language in these closing phrases, with the famous sentence (written by Chief Justice Chase) at the end of President Lincoln's final Proclamation of January 1, 1863, is remarkable.

Governor Andrew's letter of September 22, which has been quoted, contains, perhaps, the nearest approach to political partisanship which he manifested during the whole war; and nothing save the opposition of the "citizens'" party, so called, in Massachusetts, to the policy of emancipation, could have drawn from him even that expression. Although thoroughly identified always with the political party with which he acted, until 1848 as a Whig, from then to 1854 as a Free-Soiler, and after 1854 as a Republican, yet he was always a stranger to political intrigue. His original nomination for governor was effected (as has been alluded to) by a genuine popular impulse; and although nominated and elected as a member of the Republican party, his policy of uniting all parties and classes in the support of the war sustained him in his independence of partisan influences.    During his whole administration he never once consulted with the State Committee of his party as to any of his measures or appointments, although its chairman, Hon. William Claflin (now Lieutenant Governor of the State), was one of his closest friends.    Another close friend, but one whom no consideration of friendship ever restrained from telling unpalatable truths, and whose testimony thus has an added value (Hon. Francis W. Bird, who for some years was a member of his Executive Council), has recorded his impressions of this trait of the Governor's administration, in a series of interesting personal reminiscences as follows: —

" Governor Andrew had no ' kitchen cabinet.' By this I mean that the influence of any man or any set of men could never be traced as controlling or materially affecting his policy or acts. He had, indeed, a remarkable faculty of finding the best men in the State to aid him in regard to any special measure; and undoubtedly he availed himself very largely of the assistance of such men; but the methodizing, the organizing, the concentrating of the different materials, was always his own work. With original and independent ideas and convictions of his own upon the ultimate solution of our national controversy, he was in no danger of losing sight of the great end. At the same time, he recognized the fact that there were many men about him superior to himself in practical capacity to deal with methods, some in one department, some in another; but the superiority of those men upon special matters gave them no right to control his general policy; and I think they never did.

" The same is true in regard to appointments to office, both military and civil. No magistrate could apply himself more carefully, laboriously, and conscientiously, in filling any responsible position, to find the right man for the right place; and while, in making appointments, he forgot himself absolutely, if it was possible for a human being to do so; literally, as he used to say, never making an appointment to suit himself; and while it always rejoiced him to oblige his friends, still no importunities of the dearest friends could induce him to make an appointment or recommend a measure which did not accord with his sense of public duty; and I feel safe in saying that neither his worst enemies, nor his friends who may at times have felt disappointed or aggrieved by his decisions against their recommendation, ever soberly believed that he acted under improper influences from any set or clique ; and that, looking back over his whole administration, they cannot detect the influence of any one person or set as more potential or more constant than that of any other.''

Besides, he was avowedly adverse to all secret societies, whether of a social, or charitable, or religious, or political nature.    In a letter which he addressed in May, 1865, to a gentleman who had written to him that some persons accused him of being swayed by a connection with the Masonic order, from signing the death-warrant of Green, the Malden murderer, he said : `` I authorize you to state that I never have been, am not, and expect never to be, affiliated or connected with, or a member of, any secret society whatsoever.    Without intending to comment or reflect upon the views and action of others, I have never been able to satisfy myself of the expediency of the existence of any secret societies in a free republic.''

This independence of partisan control alienated from him all the trading politicians, and would have broken down any ordinary man in caucuses and conventions ; but he possessed a strength which was independent of small political managers. They were always against him; and the influence of almost all the old leaders of his party was against him also, from the day he was first named for governor. This last he felt keenly, and often expressed himself concerning it in private; but he was too magnanimous and public-spirited ever to resent it by reprisals upon them, although his opportunities were ample. As the world goes, it was a natural jealousy on their part. He had ridden into the lists, a stranger to the old heroes of the political tourneys of the last twenty years, and to their surprise and vexation had carried off all their accustomed prizes. During the whole war, and after his return to private life, to the day of his death, he was unquestionably the first citizen of Massachusetts in the affection of the people and the estimation of the country. This they could never brook with patience, nor could they ever comprehend the manner of it.

His unflinching exercise of the veto power also insured the opposition of that always large class of legislators who are too self-conscious of their own importance to appreciate the constitutional duty of the Executive. During his official term of five years he vetoed no less than twelve bills or resolves of the Legislature. So did his opinions concerning removals from office alienate

6

that same class of men.   Only two removals were
made by him during the five years he was governor, and in each of those cases he filed written
reasons for his action.   In a few other instances,
not half a dozen in all, he notified civil officers
of his purpose to remove them unless they should
tender their resignations, and in every instance
he specified the causes of his determination.

In his military appointments he never asked
what were the political associations of the candi-
dates, provided only they were loyal men.   General Butler, whom he designated to the command
of the Massachusetts militia sent to rescue Washington in 1861, had been the candidate of the
Breckenridge party for Governor, in opposition
to himself.   Two years after the war began, he
was not aware, in regard to half the colonels of
the Massachusetts troops, what had been their
political connections, and was quite surprised
when he was told one day, that, out of the first
fifteen colonels of three years' volunteers whom
he commissioned, only one third at the utmost
had voted for Mr. Lincoln for President, while
more than one third had voted for Mr. Breckenridge.   When it is remembered that the vote of
Massachusetts for Lincoln in 1860 was more than
one hundred and six thousand, while for Breckenridge it was only six thousand, the fact becomes more significant.

In regard to appointments over colored troops, however, he demanded not only loyalty and ability, but sympathy with that arm of the service, as a qualification. With the employment of colored men as soldiers his fame is forever identified beyond that of any other man ; and no one had a clearer conception of the logical results of that employment upon the civil and political rights generally of that class of our people. In the very first week of the war, he wrote, concerning the enrollment of colored men in the militia, that personally he knew " no distinction of class or color in his regard for his fellow-citizens, nor in their regard for our common country." In the paramount duty of allegiance owed by colored and white men alike to the national government, he found a logical and legal solution of all the technical difficulties in the way of emancipating the slaves and employing them as soldiers.

The policy of many of our commanders during the first year of the war, to expel from our military lines, if not to surrender as fugitive slaves, all colored men who there sought refuge, seemed to him not only inhuman but suicidal. He came into collision with General McClellan on the subject, at a time when that officer was at the height of his own self-confidence, and when the country was reposing in him so blind a trust that he felt emboldened to stigmatize the Governor's opinion as disloyal in presuming to differ from his own.

In the autumn of 1861, after the disastrous affair of Ball's Bluff, in which many of its gallant officers fell, and others, including its colonel and major, were made prisoners, the Twentieth Regiment of Massachusetts Volunteers remained on the Upper Potomac in a division commanded by Brigadier General Charles P. Stone, who on September 23, 1861 (just a year before President Lincoln's Emancipation Proclamation), had issued a general order (No. 16), running as follows: —

"The General commanding has, with great concern, learned that in several instances soldiers of this corps have so far forgotten their duty as to excite and encourage insubordination among the colored servants in the neighborhood of their camps, in direct violation of the laws of the United States, and of the State of Maryland in which they are serving.

"The immediate object of raising and supporting this army was the suppression of rebellion, and the putting down by military power of those ambitious and misguided people, who, unwilling to subject themselves to the Constitution and laws of the country, preferred the carrying out of their own ideas of right and wrong to living in peace and good order under the existing government. While, therefore, it should be the pride of every army to yield instant and complete obedience to the laws of the land, it is peculiarly the duty of every officer and enlisted man in this army to give an example of subordination and perfect obedience to the laws, and to show to those in rebellion that loyal national soldiers sink all private opinions in their devotion to the law as it stands."

We have made so much progress since those days that it needs effort now to realize that " the law as it stands," thus referred to, meant the Fugitive Slave Law, and that the purport of this order, in plain English, was to enjoin upon the troops to send back to their masters fugitive slaves who had taken refuge within our military lines.

During November, 1861, in filling the vacancies made by the battle of Ball's Bluff, in the roster of officers of this regiment, Governor Andrew, on the recommendation of its lieutenant-colonel, had promoted one of the lieutenants to a superior rank. Soon afterwards he was advised that this officer had been concerned in officiously returning some fugitive slaves. Immediately he wrote to the lieutenant-colonel

stating what had thus been represented, and requesting him, if the alleged facts were true, to
inform the officer thus promoted, that had those
facts been learned in season, the promotion would
never have been made.    Instead of replying to
the Governor, whether or not the alleged facts
were true (it proved afterwards that they were
not), the lieutenant-colonel forwarded the Governor's letter to General Stone, who communicated it to General McClellan ; and, all the military gentlemen mentioned having worked themselves into indignation at what they considered
the Governor's presumption, some letters passed
between him on one side, and General Mc-
Clellan on the other, in which that officer
read more honest and healthy doctrine than in
those days often came to his eyes.    The limits
of this sketch forbid the insertion of the whole
correspondence, but there is space to put on
record some extracts from the concluding letters.
That of General McClellan was dated on December 20, 1861, and he wrote : —

" In your letter the lieutenant-colonel is directed to convey censure and reprimand to an
officer of his regiment for acts performed in the
line of his military duty.    If the officer referred
to had been guilty of any infraction of military
law or regulation, the law itself points out the

method and manner for its own vindication, and the channel through which the punishment shall come. Any departure from this rule strikes immediately at the root of all discipline and subordination. The volunteer regiments from the different States of the Union, when accepted and mustered into the service of the United States, become a portion of the Federal army, and are as entirely removed from the authority of the Governors of the several States, as are the troops of the regular regiments. As discipline in the service can only be maintained by the strictest observance of military subordination, nothing could be more detrimental than that any interference should be allowed outside the constituted authorities."

And, a few days afterwards (the Governor, meanwhile, having answered the above letter), General McClellan forwarded, as if expressing more fully his own sentiments, a copy of a letter addressed to himself by General Stone, dated December 15, in which that officer had transmitted to head-quarters the Governor's letter to the lieutenant-colonel, styling it " a most extraordinary letter," and " respectfully requesting the attention of the Major-General Commanding, in the hope that he may be able to devise measures which shall in future prevent such unwarrantable and dangerous interference with the subordinate commands of the army."

After thus opening, General Stone continued : —

" The fact that most of the soldiers in the regiment referred to, were enlisted in the service of the United States, in the State of which the Governor referred to is the respected chief magistrate, does not, I conceive, give his Excellency a right to assume control of the interior discipline of the regiment, nor does it give him authority to command the punishment of a meritorious officer for any offense, either real or imaginary."

" Thousands of brave men gathered into the service of the Union (the whole Union), from five or more different States of the Union, are now serving in this division, and enduring unmurmuringly cold, hardship, and fatigue, simply because ambitious State officials at the South have unconstitutionally and lawlessly used their power to wrest from United States' officials the trusts confided to them by the nation. The usurpations of these ambitious State authorities commenced in much smaller matters than this, of assuming authority in a national regiment serving in the field against the public enemy, far removed from the State of which his Excellency is Governor ; and it matters little to me whether the usurpation comes from South or North, Georgia or Massachusetts ; I feel it my duty to bring the matter at once to an issue and, if possible, to arrest the evil before its natural fruits (open rebellion) shall be produced.

" The course of Major Anderson, one year since, in refusing to permit interference in the internal affairs of his command in Fort Sumter, on the part of the Governor of the State in which he was serving the Union, was eminently distasteful to the Governor of South Carolina ; nevertheless, Major Anderson's sense of duty prevented him from fulfilling that Governor's desires. Disagreeable as it may be to me to do anything distasteful to the Governor of any State of the Union, I do not feel that it is consistent with my sworn duty to permit any Governor to give orders affecting the discipline of any regiment which the Government of the Nation has entrusted to my command. I am not aware that there are here Michigan, New York, Pennsylvania, Minnesota, or Massachusetts troops. I do know that there are here United States' troops collected from all these States, and that they are carefully taught that their duty is to serve the United States honestly and faithfully against all those who set themselves in opposition to the Constitution and laws of the United States, whosoever the opposers may be.

"I will merely add, for the satisfaction which I know it will give to the Major-General Commanding, that I do not believe that in the instance of the officer referred to in the letter of the Governor, nor in any other instance, the orders of the War Department in reference to fugitive slaves have been violated by officers of this division; and I am equally happy to state that in no instance within my knowledge and recollection (with one exception), have the laws, on the same subject, of the State of Maryland in which we are serving, been violated by officers of the division. In that exceptional case the officer offending promptly retired from the service."

The "issue" to which General McClellan and General Stone thus sought to "bring the matter" was reached by a reply from the Governor, on December 30; and the whole correspondence was then laid by him before the President of the United States. In this reply, the Governor wrote: —

"This letter of Brigadier General Stone which (taken in connection with your own letter, General, to which I have already had the honor to reply), is thus adopted by you, and, at an interval of several days from my reply to yours, is thus forwarded to me without observation, as if with intentional indorsement of its statements, interpretations, and references, demands my attention.

" Claiming no merit for myself which does not pertain equally to the humblest citizen of the Republic (which, thanks be to God, still lives, the refuge and citadel of Democratic Republicanism of all the earth), I yet do proudly and serenely claim for the ancient Commonwealth over which it is my undeserved honor to preside as her Chief Executive Magistrate, and for the office which I occupy and strive to fill, and for my own administration of that office itself, the absolute right, — earned by history, — of repelling all that is said or insinuated in that letter. Without the alacrity, devotion to the Union cause, and energetic patriotism of Massachusetts, where to-day had been the Government ; in whose hands the capital ; where, indeed, the Union itself?   And where, since these troubles began, has been a person in any branch of service, who has devoted more hours of day and night to the simple, faithful, and untiring service of the President of the United States and his Department of War, in the cause of the country ?

" Bred, myself, a lawyer, and educated in the Massachusetts school, not only of patriotism but of constitutional interpretation, I have been neither ignorant nor unmindful of the limitations of power, the proper jurisdiction and rights of the Federal Government, nor, as the correspondence with that government for the past nine months most amply shows, of the complete duty and right of that government to lead, and of my own duty in aiding and following it in the support of the rights and honor of us all.  And now, at the end of my first official term, I cannot receive without a certain degree of honest resentment the more than insinuation contained in what is written by Brigadier General Stone, about ' the usurpations of these ambitious State authorities,' and the like.

" The remark of that officer that ' the fact that most of the soldiers in the regiment referred to, were enlisted into the service of the United States in the State of which the Governor referred to is the respected Chief Magistrate, does not, I conceive, give his Excellency a right to assume control of the internal discipline of the regiment, nor does it give him authority to command the punishment of a meritorious officer for any offense, real or imaginary,' is the key to all the errors of fact and inference, and of all the impertinent remark which follows.

"But, first, General, I beg to call your attention

to the attempted belittling of the Commonwealth of Massachusetts, by the implication that all she had to do with the Twentieth Regiment was, that 'most of the soldiers' were enlisted in 'the State.' The regiment was raised in the State, under my authority, in response to a certain requisition, not for *soldiers*, but for 'ten *regiments*,' from the Department of War. I appointed and commissioned its officers, and the regiment was recruited here, on our own soil, at Camp Massasoit in the town of Dedham and County of Norfolk, and marched from here to Washington with every kind of equipment and furniture recognized by the Army Regulations of the United States, and all of it provided and paid for by this Commonwealth, from its army wagons, ambulances, and horses, and its Enfield rifles (imported by Massachusetts from England under contracts made by an agent sent there by the State the next week after the fall of Sumter), down to shoe-strings and tent-pins. Nor did we omit to supply anything for which the gallant Colonel William Raymond Lee (now a prisoner in a felon's cell at Richmond), himself a regularly educated officer and distinguished graduate of West Point, suggested to me even a wish.

" I would to Heaven that he were back now at the head of his regiment; or that the Army of the Potomac were hammering at his prison-door with both hands — and neither hand averted to protect the institution which is the cause of all this woe.

" But, next, please to notice the allegation that the Governor did ' assume control of the interior discipline of the regiment,' — an averment for which the letter to the lieutenant colonel affords no shadow of justification (the propriety of which letter was fully shown in my note to you of December 24), unless I am to understand that it is wrong for Governors not to promote volunteer officers, who, in pretended obedience to army orders, break the laws in super-serviceable police work in aiding the pursuit of fugitive slaves.

" The facts of which I wrote to the lieutenant-colonel were in equal violation of the laws of the United States and of the very General Order (No. 16) issued by Brigadier General Stone himself, and now forwarded, by copy, to me ; and I had, unwittingly, promoted the officer who was subsequently reported as guilty of the wrong. Brigadier General Stone, it seems, was shown my letter to the lieutenant colonel in which I spoke of the reported conduct in the tone its illegality and inhumanity alike deserved. If the facts were not true, it was plain my letter did not apply to them nor to the officer promoted.

This Brigadier General Stone and the lieutenant colonel could see ; and they also saw and must know that my correspondence was not, either in substance or form, " a command of punishment." And the lieutenant colonel's duty, if in fact the young man had done only what he was compelled to do by superior authority, was to have informed me to that effect in reply. If otherwise, truth, justice, and duty required him to inform the officer, named in my letter to him, that I had promoted him in ignorance of what had occurred.

" I am sorry to perceive in the conduct of Brigadier General Stone and of the lieutenant colonel, a levity of mind which does not appreciate the responsibility of the grave duties with which the power of appointment charges the officer in whom it is vested."

In the spring of the same year, while the Massachusetts troops were on their way to Washington, the Governor had had occasion to define his opinions on a kindred subject in a correspondence with General Butler, who was at the time a Brigadier in command of the Massachusetts militia, and not mustered into the United States' service. On the 23d of April, 1861, while the General, with the Fifth and Eighth Massachusetts regiments, was at Annapolis, endeavoring to open communication with the beleaguered capital, one of his staff-officers, by his direction, telegraphed to the Governor that " this morning, hearing of a threatened slave insurrection, General Butler tendered the forces under his command to Governor Hicks for its suppression." It is not the purpose of this sketch to revive the difficulties which then and afterwards occurred between the Governor and General Butler ; but inasmuch as the reply of the latter to the letter which the Governor sent in answer to this dispatch was published at the time, the present seems to be a proper occasion to place on record both sides of the correspondence.

The Governor wrote on April 25, 1861 : —

" I have received through Major Ames a dispatch transmitted from Perryville, detailing the proceedings at Annapolis from the time of your arrival off that port until the hour when Major Ames left you to return to Philadelphia.

" I wish to repeat the assurances of my entire satisfaction with the action you have taken, with a single exception. If I rightly understand the telegraphic dispatch, I think that your action in tendering to Governor Hicks the assistance of our Massachusetts troops to suppress a threatened servile insurrection among the hostile people of Maryland, was unnecessary. I hope that the fuller dispatches, which are on their way from you, may show reasons why I should modify my opinion concerning that particular instance, but, in general, I think that the matter of servile insurrection among a community in arms against the Federal Union is no longer to be regarded by our troops in a political, but solely from a military point of view, and is to be contemplated as one of the inherent weaknesses of the enemy, from the disastrous operation of which we are under no obligation of a military character to guard them in order that they may be enabled to improve the security which our arms would afford so as to prosecute with more energy their traitorous attacks upon the Federal Government and Capital.

" The mode in which such outbreaks are to be considered should depend entirely upon the loyalty or disloyalty of the community in which they occur ; and in the vicinity of Annapolis I can, on this occasion, perceive no reason of military policy why a force summoned to the defense of the Federal Government, at this moment of all others, should be offered to be diverted from its immediate duty to help rebels who stand with arms in their hands obstructing its progress towards the City of Washington. I entertain no doubt that whenever we shall have an opportunity to interchange our views personally on

7

this subject, we shall arrive at entire concordance of opinion."

The General, replying on May 9, 1861, and addressing the reply to the Governor as his commander-in-chief, after defending his action in the particular instance, on the ground that by reason of it "confidence took the place of distrust, friendship of enmity, and brotherly kindness of sectional hate," so that he believed that at the time he wrote there was "no city in the Union more loyal than the city of Annapolis," continued : —

"But I am to act hereafter, it may be, in an enemy's country, among a servile population, where the question may then arise as it has not yet arisen, as well in a *moral* and *Christian* as in both a *political* and *military* point of view. What shall I then do? Will your Excellency bear with me a moment while this question is being discussed? I appreciate fully the force of your Excellency's suggestion as to the inherent weakness of the rebels arising from the preponderant servile population. The question then is, in what manner shall we take advantage of that weakness? By allowing, and of course arming, that population to rise upon the defenseless women and children of the country, carrying rapine, arson, and murder, all the horrors of San

Domingo a million times magnified, among those whom we hope to reunite with us as brethren, many of whom are already so, and those worth preserving will be when this horrible madness shall have passed away or been thrashed out of them? Would your Excellency advise the troops under my command to make war in person upon the defenseless women and children of any part of the Union, accompanied by brutalities too horrible to be named? You will say, God forbid. If we may not do so in person, shall we allow others to do so over whom we can have no restraint and exercise no control, and who, when once they have tasted blood, may turn the very arms we put in their hands against ourselves as a part of the oppressive white race? The reading of history, so familiar to your Excellency, will tell you the bitterest cause of complaint which our fathers had against Great Britain in the War of the Revolution was the arming by the British ministry of the red man with the tomahawk and the scalping-knife against the women and children of the colonies, so that the phrase 'May we not use all the means which God and Nature have put in our power to subjugate the colonies?' has passed into a legend of infamy against the leader of that ministry who used it in Parliament? Shall history teach us

in vain ?    Could we justify ourselves to ourselves, although with arms amid the savage wild-
ness of camp and field we may have blunted
many of the finer moral sensibilities, in letting
loose four millions of worse than savages upon
the homes and hearths of the South ?    Can we
be justified to the Christian community of Massachusetts ?    Would such a course be consonant
with the teachings of our holy religion ?    I have
a very decided opinion upon the subject, and if
any one desires, as I know your Excellency does
not, this unhappy contest to be prosecuted in
that manner, some instrument other than myself
must be found to carry it on.

"I may not discuss the political bearings of this
topic.    When I went from under the shadow of
my roof-tree I left all politics behind me, to be
resumed only when every part of the Union is
loyal to the flag and the potency of the Government through the ballot-box is established.

"Passing the moral and Christian view, let us
examine the subject as a military question.    Is
not that State already subjugated which requires
the bayonets of those armed in opposition to its
rulers to preserve it from the horrors of a servile
war ?    As the least experienced of military men,
I would have no doubt of the entire subjugation
of a State brought to that condition.    When,

therefore, unless I am better advised, any community in the United States who have met me in honorable warfare, or even in the prosecution of a rebellious war in an honorable manner, shall call upon me for protection against the nameless horrors of a servile insurrection, they shall have it. And, from the moment that the call is obeyed, I have no doubt we shall be friends and not enemies.

"The possibilities that dishonorable means of defense are to be taken by the rebels against the Government I do not now contemplate. If, as has been done in a single instance, my men are to be attacked by poison, or, as in another, stricken down by the assassin's knife, and thus murdered, the community using such weapons may require to be taught that it holds within its own borders a more potent means for deadly purposes and indiscriminate slaughter than any which it can administer to us."

The Governor never replied to this letter. He deemed it a communication unjustifiable by anything contained in his own letter to which it purported to be in reply, and improper under any circumstances from a subordinate to his commander-in-chief; and he was impressed, rightly or wrongly, that the writer, looking forward to a speedy peace, wished to get on record something that should be available for renewing old political associations, and misconstrued his letter of April 25 for that purpose.    And this grieved him; for, giving himself up so entirely to the country's cause, and accepting, against all his own old sentiments, the instrumentalities of war, by which alone that cause could be maintained, he looked for equal self-abnegation in others.

But the ensuing year brought great changes, both in measures and in men.    On January 1, 1863, General McClellan, having lost command of the Army of the Potomac, was seeking to retrieve his fortunes by the political aid of the northern opponents of the war; and General Butler had just been superseded in command at New Orleans, after a political administration of that city in which he had been firmly supported by the Governor, notwithstanding his conduct in Massachusetts while gathering troops for the Louisiana campaign; and after which he would hardly have repeated such a letter as was his of May 9, 1861—at least not in answer to such a letter as was the Governor's of April 25.

# CHAPTER VII.

He obtains official sanction of the Federal Government to the en-
listment of colored troops. — He raises the Fifty-fourth and
Fifty-fifth Massachusetts (colored) regiments. — Contest for their
equal rights with white troops in pay and rank. — Antagonism
with the War Department on these questions. — Appeal to the
President. — The Attorney General overrules the legal position of
the Secretary of War. — Correspondence with the President. —
Correspondence with Thaddeus Stevens. — He finally triumphs
and secures the rights of his colored soldiers. — His aid of enlist-
ment of colored soldiers everywhere. — He procures organization of Freedmen's Inquiry Commission. — Services in behalf
of the freedmen. — Opposition to system of arbitrary arrests in
Loyal States. — He declines to take part in the Surratt trial.

AT last, on January 26, 1863, the official
sanction of the National Government was granted
to the raising of colored troops. At a personal interview with the Secretary of War,
that day, at Washington, concerning the coast
defenses of Massachusetts and the garrison of
Fort Warren, the Governor obtained from him
written authority to raise " volunteer companies
of artillery for duty in the forts of Massachusetts
and elsewhere, and such companies of infantry
for the volunteer military service as he may find
convenient." With his own hand the Governor

then added to the writing, after the words quoted, the further words, " and may include persons of African descent organized into separate corps," and presented it to the Secretary for his signature ; and it was signed.

Hardly daring to communicate to the authorities at Washington the extent of his purposes under this authority, for fear lest it should be revoked, he hastily returned with it to Boston, and, the very day of his arrival, began the work of raising the famous Fifty-fourth Regiment of Massachusetts Infantry at the camp at Readville. It was a proud and happy day for him, that bright May morning when it stood, complete, before the State House, the equal of the best Massachusetts regiments which had preceded it, in the quality, discipline, and equipment of the men, and the character of the officers ; and when he marched between its ranks down Beacon Street to the old parade-ground of the Common, and it passed him there in review in the presence of more than fifty thousand spectators !

The Fifty-fifth Regiment, in all respects a worthy companion of the Fifty-fourth, followed it to the field ; and, after them, was raised and sent a fine regiment of colored cavalry.  But the triumph over prejudice was not yet complete. The right of the colored soldier to equality with his white companions in arms remained to be vindicated. This, in respect to pay, the Governor effected after a long legal struggle over the case of the chaplain of the Fifty-fourth, a colored man ; and in respect to rank, after another long struggle over the cases of certain lieutenants whom he had promoted from among the enlisted men of the same corps on the recommendation of their superior officers.

In this contest for the rights of the colored troops differences arose between him and the Secretary of War, which never were reconciled. The men of the Fifty-fourth Regiment, after the bloody assault on Fort Wagner, found themselves denied by orders of the War Department, their pay as soldiers, when they came to the pay-table, but were tendered pay as cooks and ditchers and stevedores, which they unanimously refused to accept. They appealed for justification to the Governor, under whose assurances of their equal rights with all other soldiers they had been enlisted ; and he appealed to the Secretary, under whose assurances he had enlisted them, and demanded the reason for this discrimination between them and the white troops who also had been enlisted under the same order of January 26, 1863. The Secretary thereupon sheltered himself behind a legal opinion of the

Solicitor of his Department. The Governor indignantly denied the correctness of the Solicitor's law, and appealed to the President, who referred the subject to the Attorney General of the United States, Mr. Bates, who overruled the opinion of the Solicitor; and at last the men received their due, but not until after they and their families had endured indescribable misery, for more than a year intervened before their justification was complete. The Governor summoned the Legislature of Massachusetts in extra session, in the autumn of 1863, and procured an appropriation out of which to pay the Massachusetts colored regiments, in this default of the United States, and sent paymasters to South Carolina with the money; but the men refused to accept from the State as a gratuity what they claimed from the United States as a right.

The intensity of the Governor's indignation at the monstrous injustice knew no bounds. The opinion of the Attorney General, reversing that of the Solicitor, was rendered on April 23, 1864. Weeks then elapsed without any reversal by the War Department of its action. The Governor then, on May 13, 1864, appealed again to the President in the following letter : —

" COMMONWEALTH OF MASSACHUSETTS,  
BOSTON, *May* 13, 1864.

" To THE PRESIDENT OF THE UNITED STATES : —

" *Sir :* I respectfully call to the attention of your Excellency the case of the Reverend Samuel Harrison, lately chaplain of the Fifty-fourth Regiment of Massachusetts Infantry Volunteers, and to the communication which I had the honor to address to your Excellency on the twenty-fourth day of March last, and the decision of the Attorney General of the United States on the questions of law involved in the case, which decision was submitted by him to your Excellency under date of the twenty-third day of April last and concluded in the following words, namely : —

" ' Your attention having been specially called to the wrong done in this case, I am also of opinion that your constitutional obligation to take care that the laws be faithfully executed, makes it your duty to direct the Secretary of War to inform the officers of the Pay Department of the Army that such is your view of the law, and I do not doubt that it will be accepted by them as furnishing the correct rule for their action.

" ' (Signed)             EDWARD BATES,  
                                        *Attorney General.*

" (Addressed) ' To THE PRESIDENT.' "

" As a proper representative of Chaplain Harrison and also of all the non-commissioned officers and privates of the Fifty-fourth and Fifty-fifth

Regiments of Massachusetts Infantry Volunteers, the rights and interests of all of whom are involved in the settlement of the legal questions aforesaid, — after having waited during a reasonable time for the consideration of the subject by your Excellency, — I do hereby respectfully claim, and, so much as in me lies, I do by this appeal to your Excellency hereby demand, of and from the Executive Department of the Government of the United States the just, full, and immediate payment to all the aforesaid officers and men, of the sums of money now due to them as volunteer soldiers of the United States serving in the field, according to the 5th Section of the 9th Chapter of the Acts of Congress of the year 1861, placing the officers, non-commissioned officers and privates of the volunteer forces in all respects, as to pay, on the footing of similar corps of the regular army.

" Already these soldiers, than whom none have been more distinguished for toilsome work in the trenches, fatigue duty in camp, and conspicuous endurance and valor in battle, have waited during twelve months, and many of them yet longer, for their just and lawful pay.

" Many of those who marched in these regiments from this Commonwealth have been worn out in service, or have fallen in battle on James'

Island, in the assault upon Fort Wagner, or in the affair of Olustee, yielding up their lives for the defense of their native country, in which they had felt their share of oppression, but from which they never had received justice.

" Many also yet linger, bearing honorable wounds, but dependent upon public charity while unpaid by the Government of the Nation the humble wages of a soldier, and sick at heart as they contemplate their own humiliation.

" Of others, yet alive and remaining in the service, still fighting, and wholly unpaid, the families have been driven to beggary and the almshouse.

" These regiments, Sir, and others situated like these, stung by grief and almost crazed by pangs with which every brave and true man on earth must sympathize, are trembling on the verge of military demoralization. Already one man of a South Carolina regiment raised under the orders of Major-General Hunter with the same interpretation of the laws of Congress now given by the Attorney General of the United States, has suffered the penalty of death for the military offense of mutiny by refusing further obedience to his officers, and declaring that by its own breach of faith the Government of the United States had released him from his contract of en-listment as a soldier. The Government which found no law to *pay* him except as *a nondescript or a contraband*, nevertheless found law enough to *shoot* him as *a soldier*.

"In behalf of the sufferings of the poor and needy, of the rights of brave men in arms for their country, of the statutes of Congress, and of the honor of the Nation, I pray your Excellency to interpose the rightful power of the Chief Executive Magistrate of the United States, who is bound by his oath ' to take care that the laws be faithfully executed; ' and by its immediate exercise to right these wrongs.

"I have the honor to remain

"Your Excellency's obedient servant,

"JOHN A. ANDREW,
*The Governor of the Commonwealth of Massachusetts.*"

Even again, on May 27, the Governor addressed the President, fortifying the opinion of Attorney General Bates by reference to the similar opinion of William Wirt, when Attorney General in 1823, on a similar question of legal interpretation ; but from some cause which it remains for history to disclose, the President did not, and the Secretary of War would not, act.

Even after all this there was delay of weeks,

almost of months; and finally the Governor appealed from the Administration to Congress, in a letter to Thaddeus Stevens, on June 4, 1864; which, after reciting the legal arguments he had urged upon the President and Secretary of War, for justice to the colored troops, ended with this passionate outburst : —

" It is a shame for the Administration to wait for an act of Congress, knowing now what the law really is, and what it has always been held to be, even so long ago as the days of Madison and Monroe. But, since the Administration does wait, then Congress ought to act, and by legislative voice declare the law. For one, I will never give up my demand for right and justice to these soldiers. I will pursue it before every tribunal. I will present it in every forum where any power resides to assert their rights and avenge their wrongs. I will neither forget nor forgive, nor intermit my effort, though I should stand unsupported and alone ; nor though years should pass before the controversy is ended. And if I should leave this world with this work undone, and there should be any hearing for such as I elsewhere in the Universe, I will carry the appeal before the tribunal of Infinite Justice."

Under the pressure of legislation threatened in Congress, the War Department at last suc-

cumbed; and the men were paid in conformity
with the orders and the law as the Governor had
construed them from the first.   His triumph was
complete; but through what anxiety and misery
had he and his colored soldiers passed to win it!
Nevertheless, during the whole period, his zeal
for the employment of colored men as soldiers
did not relax in the slightest; for, having faith
in democratic government, he had faith in the
will of the American people to do justice on any
and every question when brought to their com-
prehension; and he believed not only that the
liberties of the colored race, but that the destinies
of the country itself were involved in this question.

So he aided in the recruiting of colored
troops everywhere; through Major Stearns in
Tennessee; through General Wild in North
Carolina; through General Ullmann in New
Orleans.   The records of the State House are
full of testimony of his constant services in this
behalf; and at the same time he was unremitting
in service generally for the freedmen.   It was in
great part through his efforts that in March, 1863,
the original Inquiry Commission, of which Robert Dale Owen was chairman, was appointed by
the War Department to examine and report upon
the condition of the freedmen then newly eman-

cipated. In all the societies organized in Massachusetts, during the ensuing months, for their care and education, he was an active participant. And when at last the Freedmen's Bureau was created, he extended constant sympathy and support to Major-General Howard. Recognizing that Massachusetts was pledged, above every other State, to defend and justify the policy of emancipation, he felt a double duty in the cause — as a magistrate and as a man.

Well might the colored citizens of Boston resolve, after his death, that " the colored soldiers and sailors will ever remember that it is to him they are indebted for equal military rights before the law; " but the poor colored women and children who ran by the side of the hearse over the whole of its long route from Boston to Mount Auburn, rendered a more touching tribute to his benefactions to their race than ever can be expressed by the most eloquent eulogy. To them and such as they he was always accessible, and his heart and hand were always open.

Besides the question of the rights of colored troops, another on which he differed widely from the course of the Central Government was as to the power of arbitrary arrest so loosely exercised in the loyal States by the Federal Secretaries of State and War; and it was through his known

8

determination to support the courts of the Commonwealth in enforcing the liberty of any citizen who should appeal to them for protection, that Massachusetts was not made a field, like some other States, for the operations of the military police of Brigadier General Baker.* Abuse of the freedom of speech, even in criticism of the government during most trying periods, was, to his mind, an evil less dangerous than its repression by unlawful power, whether of a Secretary or a mob. In his address to the Legislature the month after the beginning of the war, he said: —

" It is impossible that such an uprising of the people as we have witnessed, so volcanic in its energy, should not manifest itself here and there in jets of unreasonable passion and even of violence against individuals who are suspected of treasonable sympathies. But I am glad to believe that respect for every personal right is so general and so profound throughout Massachusetts that few such demonstrations have occurred in our community. Let us never, under any conceivable circumstances of provocation or indignation, forget that the right of free discussion of all public questions is guaranteed to every individual on Massachusetts soil, by the settled conviction of her people, by the habits of her

* The chief of the secret police of the War Department.

successive generations, and by express provisions of her constitution. And let us, therefore, never seek to repress the criticisms of a minority, however small, upon the character and conduct of any administration, whether State or National."

The very faith in the principles of democratic government which filled him with such ardor in support of the war, inspired him with apprehension of the consequences of despotic use of power by the Federal Administration; and this influenced largely his theory of the proper method of reconstruction. To such proceedings as the trial of Mrs. Surratt by military commission at Washington, in usurpation of the functions of the civil courts which were there in open exercise of appropriate jurisdiction, he was totally opposed; and when, a year later, a retainer was offered to him by the Secretary of State to conduct in behalf of the Government the trial of her son, he peremptorily refused to accept it, lest thereby he should commit himself to justifying, even indirectly, the course of procedure against the mother.

# CHAPTER VIII.

Reverence for history of Massachusetts. — Fondness of old associations. — Official dignity. — His body-guard. — Care of Harvard College. — Theories concerning education in Massachusetts.
— Schools of agriculture and mechanic arts. — Letter of Count
de Gasparin. — Views of the true future of New England. —
Testimony of Mr. Evarts and Mr. Godwin to the hopes entertained of his future national career.

THE Governor had a filial reverence for the
history of Massachusetts, and studied it faithfully. He was a member of the Massachusetts
Historical Society, and was president of the New
England Historical and Genealogical Society.
At the time of his death he was engaged in col-
lecting materials for an historical essay on the
Siege of Louisburg. Among the minor measures which he persistently urged upon the Legislature until they adopted it, was a recommendation to preserve the record of our Provincial
statutes, by transcribing a copy of them which
exists in the library of a gentleman of Norfolk
County. Few men possessed more thorough
knowledge of the unwritten history of our statute law. He was very fond of certain stately
old provisions of the Constitution of the Com-

monwealth, which in these democratic days it would hardly be possible to reënact if the Constitution were now to be framed anew ; such as the recital of reasons for establishing by law permanent and honorable salaries for the Governor and the justices of the Supreme Judicial Court, and the whole chapter concerning Harvard College. Even in little things he manifested the same love of old associations. He took an almost boyish satisfaction in discovering that there existed in the office of the State Printer an old font of type, by means of which his first Thanksgiving-day Proclamation could be printed in precisely the same style in which he had seen those of Governor Brooks and Governor Eustis when he was a boy, and when they used to be issued on a broad sheet which hung over the pulpit cushions when the preachers read them.

By virtue of the same quality of mind, although he was delightfully familiar with his official associates, and in respect to freedom of access by the public was informal beyond precedent, yet he was a lover of ceremonial, when it did not interfere with what was essential and practical. He had as keen sensibility of the dramatic as of the mirthful, and in this sensibility found a great source of inspiration. Of the dignity of his office he was a jealous guardian. No better evidence of that fact can exist than is to be found in his printed correspondence with Major-General Butler, in 1861 and 1862. In all his official intercourse with the legislative body he maintained scrupulously the traditional ceremonies. The day of the Annual Election Sermon was one of great delight to him. Marching to the Old South Church, under the escort of his body-guard and surrounded by his associates in the government of the Commonwealth, it was easy to see in his face, as he passed down the old and narrow streets, the noble consciousness that he was no unworthy successor of John Winthrop and Samuel Adams.

The sentiment which grew up between him and his body-guard was something beyond previous example. There was hardly a member of it whose official respect for him was not mingled with personal affection ; and though he had been a private citizen again for two years when he died, yet it was under their familiar escort that his mortal remains passed to their last place of rest.

This veneration for the history and traditions of Massachusetts had much to do with his earnest care of Harvard College. The fact that it was the constitutional college, so to speak, was an irresistible claim upon his official regard, and in its foundations he recognized the most available basis for building up, what the framers of the Constitution anticipated, a "University." He clearly foresaw how Massachusetts, by the limitations of its territory, must become relatively less and less powerful, man for man, than newer States of greater area. The method by which he expected to maintain the ascendency of this State against such inevitable odds, was by making the Massachusetts man count for more on the destiny of the country than the man of any other State. For this he looked to facilities for broader and deeper education here than can be obtained elsewhere in America. It is impossible to over-estimate the importance he attached to ingrafting this policy on the legislation of the State, and the regret he felt that it was not appreciated and adopted by the Legislature on the occasions when he urged it, especially in reference to the land grant of the United States for schools of agriculture and the mechanic arts. His inaugural address to the Legislature of 1863 contains a full exposition of his views on the subject, which, however, seemed to be appreciated more truly by scholars and thinkers all over the world, than by the respectable body to which they were addressed.

In illustration of the cordiality with which they

were received by our best friends in Europe many proofs might be cited from the Governor's correspondence. There is room here only for a single letter, of the Count de Gasparin; which is interesting also as a recognition by that warm friend of America, of the wisdom of the policy of reconstruction advocated by his correspondent more fully, two years later, in his valedictory address upon retiring from office at the close of the war.

" VALLEYRES, CANTON DE VAUD, }
SUISSE, 9 *Juin*, 1863. }

" MONSIEUR : Vous avez bien voulu me faire envoyer des documents que je viens de lire avec un vif intérêt, et dont j'éprouve le besoin de vous remercier.

" Quel noble histoire que celle de Massachusetts ! Quel grand rôle remplit la Nouvelle Angleterre tout entière depuis la révolte odieuse du Sud ! Je comprends bien que les champions de l'esclavage vous détestent plus par jalousie et que certaines imaginations perverties de l'Ouest rêvent une Confédération qui serait débarrassée de vous.

" Tenez bon, je vous en supplie ! Continuez à appuyer purement et simplement le gouvernement de M. Lincoln. Ne vous divisez pas ! et vous verrez que malgré quelques fautes (surtout dans la direction de la guerre) vous finirez par atteindre le but.

" Ce serait un bien grand jour, celui où l'Union serait rétablie, où l'esclavage serait definitivement aboli, où la prospérité du Sud serait fondée sur de nouvelles et plus sûres bases, où la diminution rapide de l'armée serait décrétée, où les États-Unis commenceraient à revenir vers leurs petits armées et leurs petits budgets, où les mesures de repression et de confiscation seraient abolies ! Non seulement il faut rétablir l'Union, mais il faut la rétablir au profit de la liberté ; et ce second objet est plus important encore que le premier. Si vous aboutissez à une régime de dictature militaire et d'oppression, de garnison dans le Sud, il y aurait lieu de s'affliger beaucoup.

" Mais j'ai de meilleures espérances. Je les ai surtout lorsque je vois ces adresses si remarquables où respire un sentiment de patriotisme, de liberalisme, et de vraie piété. Vous priez ! Vous regardez à Celui qui seul peut vous délivrer ! Soyez sur qu'il vous réserve de grandes bénedictions.

" Parmi les sujets que vous traitez, je suis frappé de votre projet relatif à l'enseignement supérieur agronomique. Mon pére avait donné vie à un projet pareil, mais l'Institut de Versailles a succombé sous le poids des nécessités politiques.

" Vous connaissez l'intérêt profond que m'inspirent les États-Unis.   Cet intérêt n'a pu que s'accroitre par la lecture des documents que je dois á votre obligeance.

" Permettez, Monsieur, que de loin je vous serre respecteusement la main, en priant Votre Excellence de croire à mes sentiments de haute estime et de dévouement.

" A. DE GASPARIN." *

* The following is a translation of the letter in the text : —

VALLEYRES, CANTON OF VAUD,<br>" SWITZERLAND, June 9, 1868.

" SIR:   I have just read, with a lively interest, the documents which you were so kind as to cause to be sent to me, and for which I feel the need of expressing to you my thanks.

" What a noble history is that of Massachusetts!   What a grand part all New England has played since the odious revolt of the South!   I fully comprehend how the defenders of Slavery hate you the more from jealousy, and how certain perverted imaginations in the West dream of a confederation which shall be independent of New England.

" Remain steadfast, I beg you!   Continue to support purely and simply the government of Mr. Lincoln.   *Never* divide, and in spite of some errors (especially in the management of the war) you will end by attaining your object.

" It will be indeed a great day when the Union shall be reëstablished, and when Slavery shall be definitively abolished ;   when the prosperity of the South shall be founded upon new and surer bases ;   when the rapid disbanding of the army shall be ordered ; when the United States shall once more return to their small armies and small budgets ;   when the measures of repression and confiscation shall be abolished !

"It is not only necessary to reëstablish the Union, but to reëstablish it in the interest of Liberty, and this second object is even more important than the first.   If you end by adopting a military

In an address which the Governor delivered before the New England Agricultural Society on September 9, 1864, the nature of the occasion permitted him to introduce the same subject, and to treat it more rhetorically than was possible on the previous occasion mentioned. Anticipating the end of the rebellion, he said : —

" I have not failed to perceive nor to exult in the thought of the boundless possibilities of grandeur and beneficent power which pertain to the future of our America. I do not forget that when the national jurisdiction over all our States and Territories shall resume its unquestioned sway, and our national career shall begin

dictatorship and measures of oppression such as garrisons in the South, there will be great reasons for regret. But I have better hopes, and especially when I see these remarkable addresses breathing such a sentiment of patriotism, liberality, and true piety. You pray! You look to Him, who alone can deliver you! Be sure that God reserves for you great blessings.

" Among the subjects of which you treat I am struck with your project relative to a superior agricultural instruction. My father originated a similar project, but the Institute of Versailles had to give way under the weight of political necessities.

" You know the profound interest with which the United States inspire me. This interest could only be increased by reading the documents you have obliged me by sending.

" Permit me, Sir, though at a distance, respectfully to press your hand, praying your Excellency to believe me

" With sentiments of the highest esteem

and devotion, yours, etc.,

A. DE GASPARIN."

anew, the accelerated increase of wealth and of population in their necessary distribution and diffusion will, year by year, constantly diminish the relative material strength of these Northeastern States. The broad lands, the deep soils, the cheap farms, the coal mines, the gold fields, the virgin forests, the oil wells, the cotton plant, and the sugar cane, of the West and of the South, of the Gulf and of the Pacific coast, cannot fail in their attractions. The swelling tide of immigrant populations will flow across these Atlantic borders to those alluring homes and seats of industry. Along with many better men will come the greedy adventurers, some of them ignorant, some of them sordid, unblest by filial love or patriotic sentiment, to seize the opportunities of golden fortune. The wild chase for gain, the allurements of Nature herself, the temptations of that fevered life which distinguishes the youth of society in fertile and fruitful States, containing within themselves of necessity a certain measure of social and public danger, suggest to us in advance the duty and the destiny of New England.

"She is to be, in the long and transcendent future of the Republic, the great conserving influence among the States. For nearly two centuries and a half, already, have her people kept the vestal fire of personal and public liberty brightly burning in her little town democracies. Obedient to order, and practicing industry as well as loving individual freedom, they have acquired at last an instinct which discriminates between license and liberty, between the passion of the hour and the solemn adjudications of law. They possess the traditions of liberty, they inherit ideas of government, they bear about in their blood and in their bones the unconscious tendencies of race, which rise almost to the dignity of recollections and which are more emphatic and more permanent than opinions. By the toil of more than seven generations they have acquired and hold in free tenure their titles and their possessions. The dignity of the freehold, the sacredness of the family, the solemnity of religious obligation, the importance of developing the intellect by education, the rightful authority of government, the rightfulness of property fairly earned or inherited, as flowing from the inalienable self-ownership of man and the rights of human nature; the freedom of worship, the idea of human duty, expanded and enforced by the consciousness of an immortal destiny, are alike deeply imbedded in the traditions and convictions of the immense and controlling majority of our people.

" If there is aught which men deem radical-
ism, or fear as dangerous speculation, in our
theology or our politics, I call mankind to bear
witness that there is no child so humble that he
may not be taught in all the learning of the
schools, no citizen so poor that he may not aspire
to any of the rewards of merit or honorable ex-
ertion, not one so weak as to fall below the equal
protection of equal laws, nor one so lofty as to
challenge their restraints; no church nor bishop
able to impose creed or ritual on the uncon-
vinced conscience; no peaceful, pious worship
which is unprotected by the State.   Thus liberty
stands, and the law supports liberty; popular
education lends intelligence to law and gives
order to liberty, while religion, unfettered by
human arbitration between the soul of man and
the throne of the Infinite, is left free to impress
the individual conscience with all the sanctions
of its supreme behests, and of its celestial
teachings.

" Your past history is a record of many great
lives and great actions; of men, to our way of
thinking now oftentimes found narrow and even
obstinate, but yet heroic and sincere; of generations worthy to bear along and hand down the
precious seeds from which have sprung the ideas
and institutions that give dignity and welfare to
a nation.

" Agriculturists ! Yeomen of New England !
Be faithful to her ideas, to her history, her institutions and her character. Behold and adorn
your Sparta ! Reclaim and cultivate the untilled
lands which still comprise more than two-thirds
the area of the six New England States. Deepen
and widen the foundations of your seminaries and
schools of learning ; encourage genius as well as
industry. Invite hither and hold here the profound thinkers, the patient students of nature,
those tireless watchers who wait upon the stars,
or weigh the dust upon an insect's wing. Dis-
card and discourage alike the prejudices of ignorance, and the conceits of learning. Remember
that, even to-day, there is no man so wise that
he understands the law which regulates the relation of any fertilizer to any crop ; that few have
ever observed the mystery of that wonderful influence of the first impregnation of the dam
upon the future offspring of whatever sire ; that
the origin and contagion of the cattle disease or
pleuro-pneumonia, remain hitherto without adequate scientific exploration ; that the practical
farmers and men of science all combined understand as little the destructive potato-rot which
concerns the economy of every farm and every
household, as the aborigines who first descried
the Mayflower understood of the poems of

Homer or the philosophy of Aristotle.    Not undervaluing the past achievements of science, remember how infinite the extent and variety of the conquests which yet remain to her.    Let me exhort you also to bear in mind, that the great discoverers of knowledge are like prophets, appearing but seldom, and on great occasions ; that all genius is an intellectual century-plant, and that he who would make the time great, and the people noble, must not confound the mere distribution of commonplace facts, elementary or traditional knowledge, with those conquests and acquisitions which flow from patient and original explorations.

"The uses and influence of true learning, the power which flows from its sincere cultivation, are so great and enduring, that were it a task and not all a delight, I would not cease to urge and advocate, in this presence, the duty which is imposed on a people possessing the opportunities of our own.    To all peoples, to all sections, as to each individual man, are open their separate careers.    They can forfeit their places: but they can scarcely exchange them.    You of New England may forget that you are of the stock that produced Jonathan Edwards, but you cannot make the cotton plant flourish in New Hampshire.    You may turn your backs in jealousy or disdain on Bowdoin and Dartmouth and Harvard and Brown and Yale. You may set the village sexton above Cleaveland or Silliman or Agassiz. But when you have declined the sceptre of knowledge, you have not made the Merrimac or the Connecticut navigable like the Ohio, the Missouri, the Mississippi, or the Cumberland. You will win no glory by any narrow competition, or by returning one railing word for another. Your greatness must be found hereafter where it has been found hitherto, in the highest development and cultivation of the faculties of *men.* Let thoughtless politicians propose to leave New England out in the cold, if they choose. I think the world will keep a warm place for her while Vermont leads the hemispheres in the intelligence and success of her sheep breeding, while Alvan Clark makes a telescopic object glass which is the marvel of astronomers, while the new Museum of Zoölogy at Cambridge exceeds, in the variety and extent of many important classes of specimens, the more renowned museums of London and Paris. Of what account will be the sneers at Massachusetts of those ' who hold it heresy to think,' so long as one man's labor in Massachusetts is found by the census to be as productive of real wealth as the labor of five men in South Carolina, while

9

the annual earnings of her industry exceed the annual earnings *per capita* of any other community in the world ?   Schools, colleges, books, the free press, the culture of the individual everywhere, the policy of attracting, encouraging and developing all the great qualities of the head and heart, — in a word, the production and diffusion of *Ideas*, — in these shall rest for ever the secret of your strength to maintain your true position.   I implore you to unite and not divide, in your policy.   Whenever you can create a great school or find a great professor, unite to strengthen the school and to make sure of the man.   Our system of diffusing knowledge through the local schools, our plan of distributing elementary instruction, are things of which we are sure.   But your district schools will themselves go to seed, your knowledge will become bigoted and mean, unless you remember that the encouragement of these higher institutions from which they are fed and where their teachers are themselves taught, is as needful as the creation of the head of water above the dam is to the spindle's point.

" I beg to exhort you, then, to put faith in *Ideas* ; in the orderly arrangement of knowledge ; in the power to search out the hidden things of nature ; in the practical application of the highest and largest truth to the wants and affairs of man's daily life. Lead off, representative farmers of New England, and let this dear, old, rocky homestead of thought and of liberty, remain for countless ages the fountain of generous culture, science, learning, and art! Your influence will tell then, with beneficent and forever expanding power, on the destiny of the nation. You will live — the true conservatives of the civil state and of social life — ' exempted from the wrongs of time and capable of perpetual renovation.' "

Entertaining views so clear of the future relations of New England to the Union, and devoted so loyally to its welfare, it is almost impossible to overestimate the influence he would have exerted on that future, had he been spared to that limit which we assign as the full term of human life.

Mr. William M. Evarts, addressing a meeting to commemorate his services, truly said : " We do not, I fear, sufficiently appreciate the very great position which Governor Andrew had gained for himself at the age which he had reached. In this country, in whatever pursuit we attempt success, to whatever we devote our abilities and our labors, we all do our own climbing. It will be found that in the vast area of public influence in national affairs, no man fairly

gains the position which can make him known
until he reaches the age of fifty.    Mr. Webster,
than whom no other man in our time has made a
greater personal impression of talents and of
power, was of the age at which Governor Andrew
died, when he made his speech in the Senate in reply to Hayne.    And how large a proportion of the
admirers of Mr. Webster as an orator, a statesman, and a man of intellect, date their whole
knowledge and appreciation of his eminence,
not to say his preëminence, from that manifestation of his authority and his power.

" Governor Andrew led a life, the importance
and the value of which up to this time cannot be
overestimated.    Besides his direct authority in
his own State, who can measure the influence
which he exerted over the colder natures or the
duller intelligences of the public men of other
States with whom he was brought in contact !
Yet we do not err at all when we say and feel
that up to the time of his death, to human observation, he had been preparing himself and
gaining that opinion of mankind, that fame which
after death is superior to power in life, which was
to enable him to fill a greater, a wider, and a
more useful part in the future of our country.

" All this is now disappointed.    We see that
what seemed preparatory, what seemed to be

but a collection of means and power for the greatest need of statesmanship in this country, was not so designed by Providence, unless his mantle may fall upon, unless his influence may guide, unless his spirit may imbue his countrymen for this severe trial of public virtue and ability — the process of reconstruction. But whatever may happen to us or to our country, we are sure that Governor Andrew's name and fame are safe. He will go down with the whole, complete, genuine heroic fame of Governor Samuel Adams of the Revolution, and of James Otis. Nobody shall divide his honors; none shall disparage his repute. Fortunate in his life, complete in the distinction which he had gained, useful for others, gloriously for himself, he has lived and he has died."

And, to illustrate how the appreciation of what Governor Andrew had accomplished, as well as the hope of yet greater public services from him, were common to patriotic men of every school of political construction, some of the remarks with which Mr. Parke Godwin preceded Mr. Evarts on the same occasion, may here be quoted : —

"Governor Andrew," he said, "always seemed to me one of those unusual combinations of intellect with heart that constitute the groundwork of a truly great individuality. His intellect was clear, sagacious, and strong; and his heart was at once tender and sympathetic, yet brave, hopeful, and manly; both equally comprehensive and capacious. Simple as a child in his manners; gentle as a woman in his affections; earnest as the enthusiast in his persuasions of truth, and steadfast as the martyr to his own interior faith; he was yet prudent, moderate and wise as the statesman, in his action. Indeed, without disparagement of others, I may say that Governor Andrew exhibited, in a higher degree than most men, the rare qualities that distinguish the statesman from other forms of human character. He was the statesman as the statesman differs from the mere politician on one side and the simple philanthropist on the other. With none of the politician's spirit of intrigue or self-seeking, he had more than the politician's sagacity and foresight. With all the philanthropist's benevolence and zeal, he had more discernment, providence, and wisdom than ordinarily falls to that manner of men. His sensibilities enticed and ennobled his judgment, but his judgment never surrendered the reins to his sensibilities. The fire of his love blazed high, showing the path on every side of him, but never so high as to confuse the pure light of his reason. ' The perfect lawgiver,' says Macaulay, 'is a just temper between a mere man of theory who can see nothing but general principles, and the mere man of business who can see nothing but particular circumstances.' In Governor Andrew the two extremes were happily blended. He had faith in the ideal, the infinite, the perfect, and therefore was a man of principle ; but he had knowledge also of the actual, the limited, the circumstantial, and therefore he was a man of methods. His aims were never too lofty to be practicable, and his actions never so low as to swerve from the direction of his aims. Politics with him was a science of truth, but it was at the same time an art of adjustment, of the adjustment of that which is, to that which ought to be, but by processes that are sure and therefore steady in their results, and not by jerks and leaps which exhaust themselves in the very effort. Inflexibly honest in his own convictions, his sincerity always identified him with his cause ; while his kindliness and justness won him the respect and esteem of those who hated his cause. This was because he worked by persuasion, not blows ; by the persuasions of argument and character, and not force ; by the law of love, and not the love of law or rule. In these respects he often struck me as a man of the ancient mould, of that grand pattern framed in earlier days ; of the stamp and rank of the revolutionary statesmen, the Madisons, the Hamiltons, the Jays, who saw truth and clung to it with their inmost hearts, but who did not overlook or disdain the means of making that truth effective in institutions and measures — men whose clearsighted and far-reaching vision, penetrating the difficulties of the present, expanded into a prescience of the developments of the future, for which they provided.

" How nobly were all these qualities exhibited during the brief official career of Governor Andrew ! With what marvelous foresight he had prepared his State for the war while others were yet debating whether there would be a war ! With what magnetism a single word in his dispatch concerning the Massachusetts soldiers who fell in Baltimore, that their bodies should be ' tenderly ' cared for and sent home, touched all our hearts even to tears ! How, through all the dreary and protracted struggle he was always equipped, always cheerful, and always in the advance ! How the good Lincoln knew that there was one shoulder at least upon which he could ever lean his weary hands for support ! And how, when the deadly strife was over, was the sense of justice tempered with the spirit of magnanimity, so that he prosecuted peace with the same ardor that he had prosecuted war. O, what a loss is such a man to his personal and political friends! What a greater loss to his State, which he had ruled, in Milton's words, 'with a mind extended and of the diviuest mettle!' What an incomparably greater loss still to the Nation, to whose future councils he would have brought so much of insight, prudence, generosity, courage, and justice! May we not say of him, as Fisher Ames said of Hamilton, that if we weep to think of what he was, the very soul grows liquid at the thought of what he might have been!"

## CHAPTER IX.

His sensibility. — Anxiety concerning conduct of affairs at Washington. — Causes of his death. — His cheerful and mirthful disposition. — Special subjects of study. — Favorite amusements. — Administration of domestic affairs of the State. — Opposition to capital punishment. — Communications to the Legislature. — His manuscript. — His social conversation. — His eloquence. — His pecuniary means. — He resumes practice at the bar on retiring from office, refusing various public stations. — Familiarity with the Bible. — Religious catholicity. — The return of the flags.

By nature the Governor's sympathies were strong and deep, and the instances of private distress which he was called to see during the war wore on him terribly. Gradually he became accustomed to repress external manifestations of emotion, but his sensibilities were not blunted by use. Internally he endured what only those to whom he opened his heart can ever know. Perhaps the actual wear and tear was increased by this suppression of external signs; and, besides his private sympathies, there were anxieties as to the course of public affairs which he felt keenly beyond description, but which, for the sake of the public welfare, he concealed from observation. Never shunning responsibilities, yet he was fully conscious of their weight. In illustration of this, one extract from a letter which he wrote on January 14, 1863, to his friend, Mr. Bird, may here be quoted : —

" We are not to be saved in Washington by any *machinery* whatever. We can be saved, and that after we shall have passed through a great purgation, only by a revival of the religion of patriotism, and the power of a resurrection getting its hold on our own friends who are set for the defense of the people and the truth which is their salvation. Floundering along, without clear purpose, wise, united, and practical statesmanship, without any real head, how can we be victorious ? I write to you what I dare not say aloud. I see what is terrible, and yet am not terrified. But it is well that one should not venture to say needlessly things calculated to alarm others, unless those others can administer the cure.

" The truth is, I have never found in many men in Washington what I call realizing sense, practical sagacity, and victorious faith. Numbness, flightiness, selfishness, and all sorts of littlenesses, not singular in times of general prosperity when men are not summoned to be great, but astounding at a moment when men should be giants, and pigmies should be men — these strike me always, when I visit Washington, as the qualities most apparent and the uppermost. Where is the union of noble spirits? Where the few noble and unselfish hearts, to be the universal solvent, melting all others into union? Where is the grand good sense, which is the great trait of every great person in affairs? Why! we can't pay our army even, when money is cheap and is spent like water! There is enough of contentious criticism — too much — but little of the ' pull together ' quality needed to the very existence of a party, even; much more of a people. We have very able men in Washington. But they have very little idea of what God made them for, or else He means to show how much He can do for us without their aid! Now, for one, I am bound to be patient. I think we may even have to suffer great Democratic, secession, pro-slavery political defeats; that the Republicans may have to be driven out of power, and the cause of liberty and right have to win its way back again, in travail of soul; but all these experiences will pay a recompense in the end; will help assure the great hereafter! We must make up our minds now that we are ' in for a long storm.' May God help his own to be faithful to the end!"

These causes combined with his unrelaxing toil to shorten his days. In those five years of his administration he tasted the cares and sorrows, the hopes and joys, and concentrated the labors of a century of ordinary life; and such an experience aggravated his tendency to the disease which at last was fatal. No soldier struck by a rebel bullet on the battle-field died more truly a victim to the national cause. For many years he had known that he was liable to sudden death. Twice, during the period between his first election and the end of the war, he was saved from a fatal issue of attacks similar to that from which he died, only by profuse bleedings which themselves endangered life. The first time was in December, 1860, shortly before his inauguration. The second was in 1864, when he had engaged to speak, in behalf of the reëlection of President Lincoln, to mass-meetings in all the principal towns on the line of the New York Central Railroad, from Albany to Buffalo, but was compelled to desist before completing the route. But this knowledge did not depress him, nor did it ever induce him to seek for personal ease or relaxation of toil, at the cost of others.

One great source of consolation and relief he possessed in a naturally mirthful disposition. It was more than cheerful : it was merry.    He had as quick and lively perception of the ludicrous as President Lincoln himself, and his anecdote was free from coarseness.    Of the Yankee dialect he was a master.    He had studied it analytically, just as he studied the intricacies of the typical Yankee character.    The every-day life of the country villages of New England, of their shops, farm-yards, stage-coaches, taverns, sewing-circles, and household firesides, was familiar to him in all its details, and served him constantly for illustrations of stories which he told with a hearty enjoyment it excites a smile to remember.    This mirth was so natural that it sought and found material for its exercise in all the affairs of his daily business, serious or trivial ; but it never betrayed him into levity, nor was it tinged in the slightest degree with sarcasm, although it was often full of satire.    It helped him greatly to be indifferent to little mishaps and annoyances, of which, during his whole administration, there was a daily multitude that would have vexed and perplexed any man of less animal vigor and buoyant spirit.

He had a good voice and ear for music ; but all the musical training he ever enjoyed was that of the village singing-school.    It was enough, however, to encourage him always to join and often to take the lead in congregational singing, and his earnestness always carried him safely through the psalm-tunes, and the others with him. Like all simple and enthusiastic natures, his was easily stirred by melody. He delighted in martial music ; and no school-boy ever trained along through village streets by the side of the brass-band at the parade of a militia company with more charmed ear than he. But this taste was never far cultivated. He had little scientific acquaintance with the theory of music ; although, curiously enough, he possessed a minute knowledge of the history of the development of the piano-forte, of which, through some odd fancy, he had made a special study. His knowledge of this and of some other specialties, not connected with his official or professional life, afforded him often much amusement by the surprise they caused. One day, last summer, a friend was relating to him a curious incident, illustrating the theory of spiritualism, connected with an old spinnet, still preserved at Paris, which once belonged to a favorite musician at the court of Henry III. of France. In explanation of the incident the narrator was exhibiting some photographs of the instrument, and describing its construction, when, to his astonishment, he found that the Governor was even more familiar with all the details of it than he was himself.

In his address to the medical students, from which, in this sketch, some quotations have already been made, speaking from his own experience, he said : —

" The concurrent pursuit of some department of learning not in the direct line of your professional necessity I hold to be wanted for the integrity and health of your own minds. It calms, elevates, restores the jaded powers, clears the intellect, cools the judgment, and raises the moral tone. It makes life less a drudgery, and more a liberty and a joy. From morbid anatomy; from human physiology which you must perforce study always in connection with disease; from the thought of sick men and mortality, turn aside for some precious moments every day, and be devout, happy scholars and freemen of the universe ! "

His favorite amusement was to drive far out into the country around Boston with some intimate friend, and at last, when clear of the thickly settled suburbs, leaving the horse to travel almost at his own will, to abandon himself to a hilarity than which none could be more simple and genuine. Driving thus in the fresh spring air along the beautiful roads of Watertown or

Newton, fringed and fragrant with apple blossoms, he would overflow with a spring-tide of anecdote and humor. But he allowed himself few such holiday hours. Almost all his excursions from the city combined an element of business with what pleasure they afforded. Was it a sleigh-ride on a clear, crisp, Sunday morning in January; the object would be to attend the dedication of a soldiers' chapel at the Readville Camp, or the services in the chapel of the State Prison, or to sit for an hour by the bedside of some invalid soldier. Was it a drive into the green of the country, in the twilight of a summer evening; the horses would not turn their heads homeward without first stopping at the State Arsenal in Cambridge, the United States Arsenal at Watertown, the camps at Brook Farm or Medford, or the State charitable institutions at South Boston.

After the first year of the war he was accustomed to travel a good deal through the State in the summer season, but always on some official task which robbed him of a great part of the pleasure of the journey; and more than half the time he travelled by night, so as to save the daylight for business. On these excursions he would attend the Commencements at Amherst and Williams Colleges, the Wesleyan Academy,

10

and the College of the Holy Cross; inspect the work on the Hoosac Tunnel; be present at the Agricultural Fairs, and the closing of the terms of the Normal Schools; examine insane hospitals, alms-houses, jails, and houses of reformation and correction; besides visiting the numerous military camps, at Pittsfield, Greenfield, Springfield, Worcester, Groton, Wenham, Lynnfield, and Lakeville, and the great camp at Readville. How delightful he made these journeys to others, by his shrewd observation, lively wit, unfailing good temper, and ardor for everything that was charitable or patriotic, the happy recollections of those who had the privilege of being his companions will forever attest. As a rule, he disliked to talk in railroad cars. He was fond of occupying hours of railway travel with committing to memory English verses; and this is the explanation of his facility of poetical quotation. One summer, in this way, he committed to memory the whole of Mr. Longfellow's selection of minor poems, the "Waif." And he used to employ these hours also with comparing, in his own mind, his observations of the public institutions under his care, and drawing from them some wise generalization, which he rarely failed, at last to apply to some practical purpose.

His administration of the domestic affairs of

the State was as remarkable as that of its relations to the Union. The Board of State Charities was instituted, on his recommendation, for
the purpose of effecting uniformity -in the organization, discipline, and expenditures of the
various charitable and reformatory institutions.
The repeal of a constitutional amendment impos-
ing disabilities on adopted citizens was accomplished at his instance. The militia laws were
revised and amended. A system for improving
the long neglected but very valuable public
property in the flats which might be redeemed
from the sea, was projected. The policy of
increasing facilities for railroad communication
with the Northwest and the Northeast was dili-
gently fostered.

For all his communications to the Legislature
and his formal addresses to public bodies, he
made elaborate preparation, and freely commanded and used the work of others in their
details. Burdened as he was with care, it would
have been impossible for this to be otherwise.
Whether preparing for a professional argument
or an official message, he was fond of laying in
supplies and carefully organizing and drilling his
forces before beginning to move, and then of
moving *en masse.* At the time he died he had
already begun to prepare a scheme of testimony

and argument for such an elaborate attack upon the system of capital punishment, which he was planning to make before a committee of the present Legislature.

He had the habit of sending his manuscript to the printer with the various sheets pasted together into a long roll like a mammoth petition; and he made revisions in the proofs with a freedom which drove the compositors to despair. The handwriting, though bold and flowing, was far from legible; and his signature, towards the end of his official life, became a puzzle to strangers. He made a practice of signing, himself, almost all the correspondence of his office. One summer, having (with his usual pains to satisfy even trivial inquiries) replied, over his own signature, to the request of a country schoolmistress to be informed, three months in advance, what day he would appoint for Thanksgiving, she sent back the letter with a suggestion that when replying to " a woman," he should write himself instead of sending the letter of some secretary whose name she could not read. His fair correspondent had better cause of complaint about the day than about the handwriting, for, that year, the Governor, attracted by the fact that the third Thursday of November was the anniversary of the signing of the compact on board the Mayflower, designated it for Thanksgiving; and the next day after his Proclamation he received a multitude of indignant letters from pedagogues, of either sex, all over the State, whose vacations had been planned upon a presumed appointment of the last Thursday of the month, according to a time-honored custom from which he never afterwards ventured to depart, for (he used often laughingly to say) that morning's mail contained more abuse better expressed than any other he ever received.

His social talk was just like his speech in public. His public speeches, at least those made without preparation, were often effective, for this very reason, beyond the degree which the written reports of them seem to justify, if judged by a rigid standard of classical style. The natural exuberance of his language and the heartiness of his manner made him remarkably successful as an *impromptu* speaker; and it will be hardly possible for those who never knew or heard him to appreciate the wonderful influence which he exercised, through this faculty, during the war.* Hardly a day passed, certainly never

* As an example of this, Lieutenant Colonel Wilder Dwight, of the Second Massachusetts Regiment, who fell at Antietam, the Sidney of our Massachusetts youths, once told the writer that he never went under fire without repeating to himself the words with which the Governor described to the Legislature the uprising of

a week passed, during his administration, without some call for its use, and he never failed to win and command the audience, whether the occasion was a recruiting meeting, the departure of a regiment, the anniversary of a college, the morning exercises of a Sunday-school, the religious services at a prison, the " love feast " at a camp-meeting, or the festivities of a dinner-table. If the test of eloquence is success in exciting emotion at the will of the speaker, he was, throughout the war, one of the most eloquent of men ; but unquestionably a great part of this influence was due to the events of the time, and the universal admiration of his public career, which predisposed every audience to be moved by his presence. By the critical tests of oratory, one would hesitate to call him a great orator. He will be ranged with that class of public speakers of which John Bright is an eminent representative ; and many of the secrets

the country after the fall of Sumter: " The guns pointed at Fort Sumter on the twelfth day of April, while they reduced the material edifice and made prisoners of its garrison, announced to Anderson and his men their introduction into the noble army of heroes of American history ; and the cannon of the fort, as they saluted the American flag when the vanquished garrison — unconquerable in heart — retired from the scene, saluted the immortal Stripes and Stars, flaming out in ten times ten thousand resurrections of the flag of Sumter, on hill-top, staff and spire, hailed by the shouts and joyful tears of twenty millions of freemen."

of the power and charm of the two men were the same. Some of his addresses, made after careful preparation, and many of his sayings in *impromptu* speeches, will endure as long as the history of Massachusetts.

His pecuniary means were always small; so that he was debarred from an extensive exercise of private hospitality, and less of official business was associated with his domestic life than is often the case with men so genial. At the time when he became Governor his professional practice, ill-paid through many previous years, had recently begun to be lucrative. But his term of public service was so long, and its duties had been so absorbing, that when he retired from office in January, 1866, his circle of clients was entirely broken up, and he felt a reluctance to resume former professional pursuits, which only the pressure of necessity enabled him to overcome. Besides, he needed rest; and, had his circumstances permitted the leisure to enjoy it, his life might have been spared. But the bar offered the field in which to earn most surely and honorably the competency needed for his family. So, declining a proposal of the presidency of Antioch College, in Ohio; and also the offer gracefully made to him by his successor, Governor Bullock, of a seat on the bench of the Supreme Court of the State;

and declining also a commission from the Federal
Government to go to England and France, to institute proceedings in behalf of the United States,
in the courts of those countries, to compel the surrender of Confederate property, he resumed professional life at Boston ; and with such success
that when he died he was gathering its largest
pecuniary rewards as well as its highest honors.
Had he been willing, he might have retired upon
a national office comparatively a sinecure ; but he
reserved himself for more worthy duties.   The
office of Collector of Customs of the port of Boston
fell vacant at the end of the war, and an intimation was conveyed to him from the President of
the United States that if he would accept it, the
President would be glad to appoint him ; but he
instantly rejected the suggestion, and the place
was then filled by the appointment of Mr. Hamlin, whose term of service as Vice President had
recently expired.   Conversing with a friend on
the subject soon afterwards, the Governor re-
marked that it was the most lucrative public
office in the New England States, and as it had
been the habit to intrust it to men who had held
other high official stations and rendered large
public service for inadequate pay, he supposed it
was tendered to him in accordance with that
practice ; " but," added he, " I can accept no

such place for such a reason. As Governor of Massachusetts I feel that I have held a sacrificial office, that I have stood between the horns of the altar and sprinkled it with the best blood of this Commonwealth — a duty so holy that it would be sacrilege to profane it by any consideration of pecuniary loss or gain."

Metaphorical language like this, gathered from the Testaments, was as natural on his lips as if he were himself an Oriental. Few laymen were more familiar with the Bible, or had studied it with a more earnest spirit of devout criticism. The beautiful interpretation of the miracle of Cana, which he gave in his argument on the prohibitory liquor law in reply to the version of the clergyman who had argued the other side of the question, is a fine illustration of this familiarity, and of the catholicity of his religious doctrines. He was always a member of the Unitarian body of Christians, and for many years was the official head of its lay organization ; but no man was less a sectarian in creed or practice. His face was well known in places of worship of every denomination. His three closest clerical friends were his Unitarian pastor, a Roman Catholic priest, and Father Taylor, the Methodist preacher to the sailors. One Easter morning he had agreed to go with his secretary to service at a Roman

Catholic church, and that gentleman, when he called for him at the appointed hour, received a hastily written note, stating that he might be found at the little Quaker meeting-house in Milton Place, where he had gone to listen to his dear friend, Mrs. Rachel Howland.

Scores of illustrations of this catholic spirit might be written but for trespassing upon the province of his biographer. A faithful biography of Governor Andrew will be a complete history of Massachusetts during the civil war ; not alone of its connection with the war, but of all its domestic affairs, none of which escaped his anxious care. It has been the only design of the present writer, while sketching familiarly and affectionately, not so much the substance as the manner of his official life, to show how, even in little things, he exerted the same strong personal magnetism by which he inspired the people of Massachusetts in his greater acts, and how with him always, in all things, little or great, the spirit was everything, the letter nothing.

His final term as Governor expired January 5, 1866, five years to a day from the date of his first inauguration. On December 22, 1865, the anniversary of the landing of the Pilgrims at Plymouth, the flags of the hundred Massachusetts regiments and batteries which he had organized for the war, were borne through the streets of the capital of Massachusetts by the veterans who had survived the conflict, and were delivered to the hands of the Governor at the State House.

In delivering them, Major-General Couch, the commander of the column, said : —

" MAY IT PLEASE YOUR EXCELLENCY : We have come here to-day as the representatives of the army of volunteers furnished by Massachusetts for the suppression of the rebellion, bringing these colors in order to return them to the State which intrusted them to our keeping. You must, however, pardon us if we give them up with profound regret — for these tattered shreds forcibly remind us of long and fatiguing marches, cold bivouacs, and many hard-fought battles. The rents in their folds, the battle-stains on their escutcheons, the blood of our comrades that has sanctified the soil of an hundred fields, attest the sacrifices that have been made, the courage and constancy shown, that the nation might live. It is, sir, a peculiar satisfaction and pleasure to us that you, who have been an honor to the State and Nation, from your marked patriotism and fidelity throughout the war, and have been identified with every organization before you, are now here to receive back, as the State custodian of her precious relics, these emblems of the devotion of her sons. May it please your Excellency, the colors of the Massachusetts Volunteers are returned to the State."

The Governor replied : —

" GENERAL : This pageant, so full of pathos and of glory, forms the concluding scene in the long series of visible actions and events in which Massachusetts has borne a part, for the overthrow of rebellion and the vindication of the Union.

" These banners return to the Government of the Commonwealth through welcome hands. Borne, one by one, out of this Capitol, during more than four years of civil war, as the symbols of the Nation and the Commonwealth, under which the battalions of Massachusetts departed to the field, — they come back again, borne hither by surviving representatives of the same heroic regiments and companies to which they were intrusted.

" At the hands, General, of yourself — the ranking officer of the Volunteers of the Commonwealth (one of the earliest who accepted a regimental command under appointment of the Governor of Massachusetts) — and of this grand column of scarred and heroic veterans who guard them home, they are returned with honors becoming relics so venerable, soldiers so brave, and citizens so beloved.

" Proud memories of many a field ; sweet memories alike of valor and friendship ; sad memories of fraternal strife ; tender memories of our fallen brothers and sons, whose dying eyes looked last upon their flaming folds ; grand memories of heroic virtues sublimed by grief ; exultant memories of the great and final victory of our Country, our Union, and the Righteous Cause ; thankful memories of a deliverance wrought out for human nature itself, unexampled by any former achievement of arms — immortal memories with immortal honors blended, twine around these splintered staves, weave themselves along the warp and woof of these familiar flags, war-worn, begrimed, and baptized with blood.   Let ' the brave heart, the trusty heart, the deep, unfathomable heart,' in words of more than mortal eloquence, uttered though unexpressed, speak the emotions of grateful veneration for which these lips of miné are alike too feeble and unworthy.

" General : I accept these relics in behalf of the People and the Government.   They will be preserved and cherished, amid all the vicissitudes of the future, as mementoes of brave men and noble actions."

## CHAPTER X.

Valedictory address. — Description of the occasion. — He opposes
political proscription, whether of white or of black men. — He is
not in accord with either President or Congress. — Course of
public temper comes to correspond with his opinions. — Expec-
tations of his connection with the next Federal Administration.
— His natural capacity for leadership. — His estimate of the
character of President Lincoln. — Comparison of his own character with that estimate.

ONE more duty performed, his official career
was complete. Retiring from office, he delivered to the Legislature that valedictory address
on which, more than on any other production of
his pen, rests his claim to the fame of a great
statesman. Mr. James Freeman Clarke, describing the scene, says : " Who that was present can forget that last day in office ? He invited to his rooms a large number of his friends
to go in with him and hear it. There you saw
together a memorable company. There were
men and women of all ages, from Levi Lincoln,
then eighty-four years of age, to little boys and
girls. Side by side were old abolitionists and
old conservatives, orthodox men and radicals, —
those who had never met before in one room in

their lives. It seemed like the scene which will be witnessed at the Resurrection of the Just. It was on this occasion that he showed himself to be, not the fanatic he was believed to be by the Southerners, but their best friend. And it was at this time that he used the expression that having formerly urged a vigorous prosecution of the war, he should now insist on a ' vigorous prosecution of peace.' "

First, he enumerated the contributions of Massachusetts to the national cause — 159,165 soldiers and sailors in the Federal armies or navies, besides $27,705,109 appropriated from the treasury of the Commonwealth, in addition to the expenditures of the cities and towns. Then, asserting the right of Massachusetts to an influential voice in the determination of the great questions of national statesmanship raised by the issue of a war won by such sacrifices, he argued at length the terms of pacification which Massachusetts should advocate. In his view, we could not reorganize political society in the Rebel States, with any proper security, unless, first, " we let in *the people* to a coöperation, and not merely an arbitrarily selected portion of them ; " nor unless, second, " we give those who are by their intelligence and character the natural leaders of the people, and who surely will lead them by and by, an opportunity to lead them now." And he advocated the policy of settling the question of suffrage, so far as regards the voting for President, Vice President, and Representatives in Congress, by an amendment of the Federal Constitution, and, so far as regards the popular choice of all other officers in the Rebel States, by provisions of their State Constitutions, of general application, instead of leaving the subject to the shifting and inconsistent ordinary legislation of the States severally.    To the question so often asked during the two years after Governor Andrew retired from public life, Did he agree with Congress or with the President, in the strife which raged between them? these propositions render a clear reply.    The action of neither was satisfactory to him ; and he awaited patiently, in private life, the day when experience should vindicate the position he was so early to discern and so intrepid to assume.

That the course of the public temper is now in accord with his views, and that their indorsement by the people at the next election of President would have summoned him from his retirement to adorn and ennoble a national office of next to the highest honor, is a common assertion since his death.    That Massachusetts, in losing him, lost that one of her citizens whose ties of sympathy with public men of other sections of the Union were more nearly universal than those of any other, is a fact quite as generally recognized.

He was, by nature, a leader of men. There are characters whose combination of qualities, though so admirable and harmonious that their fame is well assured, yet are not sources of enthusiasm to the ordinary mass of mankind. Such a character George Washington has become in history; like Tennyson's description of the face of Maud, " faultily faultless; dead perfection, no more." None such was Governor Andrew. And there are other admirable historical characters, not so far removed from ordinary mankind as to be exalted above the plane of human sympathy, but whose great acts, which will influence countless generations, were compelled rather than original, forced upon them in the march of events rather than shaped by noble impulses of their own minds. Such a character was Abraham Lincoln. But Governor Andrew was of a different sort.

It is interesting to-day to turn back to his estimate of Lincoln as expressed in the address in which he communicated to the Massachusetts Legislature the tidings of the assassination of the President.* After describing him as the

* The last official communication from Governor Andrew to Pres-

11

man " on whom the people hung with fonder hope and confidence than had ever been exercised within the memory of the generation to which we belong," and who had added " martyrdom itself to his other and scarcely less emphatic claims to human veneration, gratitude, and love ; " and after alluding to the closeness of their personal and official relations, the Governor analyzed Lincoln's character thus : —

" I desire on this grave occasion to record my sincere testimony to the unaffected simplicity of his manly purpose, to the constancy with which he devoted himself to his duty, to the grand fidelity with which he subordinated himself to his country, to the clearness, robustness, and sagacity of his understanding, to his sincere love of truth, his undeviating progress in its faithful pursuit, and to the confidence which he could not fail to inspire in the singular integrity of his virtues and the conspicuously judicial quality of his intellect.

" He had the rare gift of discerning and setting aside whatever is extraneous and accidental, and

ident Lincoln was a telegram, dated at Boston, April 11, 1865, urging the President to proclaim a National Thanksgiving for the capture of Richmond and the final victory of Grant, and suggesting April 19, the anniversary of Lexington and Baltimore, as an appropriate day. But on April 19 the Governor was attending the funeral ceremonies for the President in the East Room of the White House at Washington.

of simplifying an inquiry or an argument by just discriminations. The purpose of his mind waited for the instruction of his deliberate judgment; and he was never ashamed to hesitate, until he was sure that it was intelligently formed. Not greatly gifted in what is called the intuition of reason, he was nevertheless of so honest an intellect that by the processes of methodical reasoning he was often led so directly to his result that he occasionally seemed to rise into that peculiar sphere which we assign to those who, by original constitution, are natural leaders among men."

And, after completing this analysis, and " challenging all human history to produce the name of a ruler more just, unselfish, or unresentful than Abraham Lincoln," the Governor continued : —

" It were premature for us to assert how, or how far, during the four years of his administration, he *led* this American People. The unfolding of events in the history we are yet to enact will alone determine the limits of such influence. It is enough for his immortal glory that he faithfully *represented* this people, their confidence in democratic government, their constancy in the hour of adversity, and their magnanimity in the hour of triumph."

" Comparing his declarations of purpose and of inclination with the great actions of his ca-

reer, we recognize how that career was shaped
by external more than by internal forces.   Until
long after his inauguration he never proposed
or counted upon war.   He proposed only to
hold, occupy, and possess the places and the
property which were within the exclusive jurisdiction of the United States.   And yet he waged
to a successful issue a civil war the most tremendous which history records.   Nor had he
ever proposed or inclined to interfere with slavery in the States.   He proposed only to check
its spread and suppress its existence in places
within the exclusive jurisdiction of the Federal
Union.   And yet he proclaimed liberty to three
millions of American slaves, and prepared the
way for Universal Emancipation.

" Without disparagement, then, of his loftiness
of motive and fullness of achievement, and without detraction from the measure of his glory,
may we not recognize in his career a Direction
Supreme above the devices or conceptions of
man, and seeing thus how a Divine Hand has
led us through these paths of trial, yield con-
fidingly to its guidance in all future years."

Reviewing the career of Governor Andrew
himself, may we not ascribe to him all the positive noble qualities with which his judgment
thus invested President Lincoln, and that inde-

finable something more, which he calls the
" intuition of reason," but let us call " inspiration ; " which is not shaped by the present, but
is of and for all time, and itself shapes the
future. Comparing his declarations of purpose
with the great actions of his administration, do
we not recognize that his career was controlled
from within, not from without ; and that the
good he did was good he planned ?

Premature as seems his death, yet he lived
long enough to leave a fame as enduring as shall
be the Commonwealth he governed. Of all his
illustrious predecessors no one achieved more
" to form a more perfect Union, establish justice,
insure domestic tranquillity, provide for the common defense, promote the general welfare, and
secure the blessings of liberty to ourselves and
our posterity." He made the first preparations
for the war and received at its close the triumphant standards of the army he organized to
wage it. " He ordered the overcoats, and he
received the flags ! " Every Massachusetts man
knows the glorious history comprised in that
brief sentence. Of his departure after such toil
and such success one well may use the verses of
the Samson Agonistes, those favorite verses
which he himself selected for the inscription on

the monument at Lowell of the first martyrs of
the war : —

> " He to Israel
> Honor hath left, and freedom, let but them
> Find courage to lay hold on this occasion;
> To himself and father's house eternal fame;
> And, which is best and happiest yet, all this
> With God not parted from him, . . . .
> But favoring and assisting to the end.
> Nothing is here for tears, nothing to wail
> Or knock the breast, no weakness, no contempt
> Dispraise or blame, nothing but well and fair,
> And what may quiet us in a death so noble."

# VALEDICTORY ADDRESS

OF

## HIS EXCELLENCY JOHN A. ANDREW,

TO THE

TWO BRANCHES OF THE LEGISLATURE OF MASSACHUSETTS,
UPON RETIRING FROM THE OFFICE OF GOVERNOR
OF THE COMMONWEALTH, JANUARY 5, 1866.

———◆———

GENTLEMEN OF THE SENATE
AND THE HOUSE OF REPRESENTATIVES: —

The People of Massachusetts have vindicated alike their intelligence, their patriotism, their will, and their power; both in the cultivation of the arts of Peace, and in the prosecution of just and unavoidable War. At the end of five years of executive administration, I appear before a convention of the two Houses of her General Court, in the execution of a final duty.

For nearly all that period, the Commonwealth, as a loyal State of the American Union, has been occupied, within her sphere of coöperation, in helping to maintain, by arms, the power of the nation, the liberties of the people, and the

rights of human nature. Having contributed to
the Army and the Navy — including regulars,
volunteers, seamen and marines, men of all arms
and officers of all grades, of the various terms
of service — an aggregate of one hundred and
fifty-nine thousand one hundred and sixty-five
men ; and having expended for the war, out of
her own treasury, twenty-seven million seven
hundred and five thousand one hundred and nine
dollars, besides the expenditures of her cities and
towns, she has maintained, by the unfailing energy and economy of her sons and daughters,
her industry and thrift, even in the waste of
war. She has paid promptly, and *in gold,* all
interest on her bonds, including the old and the
new, guarding her faith and honor with every
public creditor, while still fighting the public
enemy ; and now, at last, in retiring from her
service, I confess the satisfaction of having first
seen all of her regiments and batteries, save two
battalions, returned and mustered out of the
Army ; and of leaving her treasury provided
for, by the fortunate and profitable negotiation
of all the permanent loan needed or foreseen ;
with her financial credit maintained at home and
abroad, her public securities unsurpassed, if
even equaled, in value in the money markets of
the world, by those of any State or of the Nation.

I have already had the honor to lay before the General Court, by special message to the Senate, a statement of all affairs which demand my own official communication ; and it only remains for me to transfer, at the appropriate moment, the cares, the honors, and the responsibilities of office, to the hands of that eminent and patriotic citizen on whose public experience and ability the Commonwealth so justly relies.* But, perhaps, before descending, for the last time, from this venerable seat, I may be indulged in some allusion to the broad field of thought and statesmanship to which the war itself has conducted us. As I leave the Temple where, humbled by my unworthiness, I have stood so long, like a priest of Israel sprinkling the blood of the holy sacrifice on the altar, I would fain contemplate the solemn and manly duties which remain to us who survive the slain, in honor of their memory and in obedience to God.

The Nation, having been ousted by armed Rebellion of its just possession, and of the exercise of its constitutional jurisdiction over the territory of the Rebel States, has now at last, by the suppression of the Rebellion (accomplished by the victories of the national arms over those of the

* His Excellency, Alexander H. Bullock, the present Governor of the Commonwealth.

rebels), regained possession and restored its own rightful sway. The Rebels had overthrown the loyal State governments. They had made war against the Union. The government of each Rebel State had not only withdrawn its allegiance, but had given in its adhesion to *another*, namely, the Confederate Government — a government not only injurious by its very creation, but hostile to, and in arms against, the Union, asserting and exercising belligerent rights, both on land and sea, and seeking alliances with foreign nations, even demanding the armed intervention of neutral powers.

The pretensions of this " Confederacy " were maintained for four years, in one of the most extensive, persistent, and bloody wars of History. To overcome it and maintain the rights and the very existence of the Union, our National Government was compelled to keep on foot one of the most stupendous military establishments the world has ever known; and probably the same amount of force, naval and military, was never organized and involved in any national controversy.

On both sides there was *War*, with all its incidents, all its claims, its rights, and its results.

The States in rebellion tried, under the lead of their new Confederacy, to conquer the Union ;

but in the attempt they were themselves conquered.

They did not revert by their rebellion, nor by
our conquest, into " Territories." They did not
commit suicide. But they rebelled ; they went
to war ; and they were *conquered.*

A " Territory " of the United States is a possession, or dependency, of the United States,
having none of the distinctive, constitutional at-
tributes of a State. A Territory might be in
rebellion ; but not thereby cease to be a Territory. It would be properly described as *a Territory in rebellion.*

Neither does a State in rebellion cease to be a
State. It would be correctly described as *a
State in rebellion.* And it would be subject to
the proper consequences of rebellion, — both
direct and incidental, — among which may be
that of military government, or supervision, by
the Nation, determinable only by the Nation, at
its own just discretion, in the due exercise of
the rights of war. The power to put an end to
its life is not an attribute of a State of our
Union. Nor can the Union put an end to its
own life, save by an alteration of the National
Constitution, or by suffering such defeat in war
as to bring it under the jurisdiction of a con-
queror. The Nation has a vested interest in

the life of the individual State. The States
have a vested interest in the life of the Union.
I do not perceive, therefore, how a State has the
power by its own action alone, without the coöperation of the Union, to destroy the continuity
of its corporate life. Nor do I perceive how
the National Union can, by its own action, without the action or omission of the States, destroy
the continuity of its own corporate life. It
seems to me that the stream of life flows through
both State and Nation from a double source;
which is a distinguishing element of its vital
power. Eccentricity of motion is not death;
nor is abnormal action organic change.

The position of the Rebel States is fixed by
the Constitution, and by the laws, or rights, of
war. If they had conquered the Union, they
might have become independent, or whatever
else it might have been stipulated that they
should become, by the terms of an ultimate
treaty of peace. But, being conquered, they
failed in becoming independent, and they failed
in accomplishing anything but their own conquest. They were still States; though belliger-
ents conquered. But they had lost their loyal
organization as States; lost their present possession of their political and representative power
in the Union. Under the Constitution they

have no means or power of their own to regain it. But the exigency is provided for by that clause in the Federal Constitution in which the Federal Government guarantees a republican form of government to every State. The regular and formal method would be, therefore, for the National Government to provide specifically for their reorganization.

The right and duty, however, of the General Government, under the circumstances of their present case, is not the single one of reorganizing these disorganized States. The war imposed rights and duties, peculiar to itself and to the relations and the results of War. The first duty of the Nation is to regain its own *power*. It has already made a great advance in the direction of its power. If ours were a despotic government, it might even now be thought that it had already accomplished the reëstablishment of its power as a government. But, ours being a republican and a popular government, it cannot be affirmed that the proper power of the government is restored, until a peaceful, loyal, and faithful state of mind gains a sufficient ascendency in the rebel and belligerent States, to enable the Union and loyal citizens everywhere to repose alike on the purpose and the ability of their people, in point of numbers and capacity, to assert, maintain, and conduct State governments, republican in form, loyal in sentiment and character, with safety to themselves and to the national whole.    If the people, or too large a portion of the people, of a given Rebel State, are not willing and able to do this, then the state of war still exists, or, at least, a condition consequent upon and incidental thereto exists, which only the exercise on our part of belligerent rights, or some of their incidents, can meet or can cure.    The rights of war must continue until the objects of the war have been accomplished, and the Nation recognizes the return of a state of peace.    It is absolutely necessary then for the Union Government to prescribe some reasonable test of loyalty to the people of the States in rebellion.    It is necessary to require of them conformity to those arrangements which the war has rendered, or proved to be, necessary to the public peace, and necessary as securities for the future.    As the conquering party, the National Government has the right to govern these belligerent States meanwhile, at its own wise and conscientious discretion, subject: *First.* To the demands of natural justice, humanity, and the usages of civilized nations; *Second.* To its duty under the Constitution, to guarantee republican governments to the States.

But there is no arbiter, save the People of the

United States, between the Government of the Union and those States. Therefore the precise things to be done, the precise way to do them, the precise steps to be taken, their order, progress and direction, are all within the discretion of the National Government, in the exercise, both of its belligerent and its more strictly constitutional functions — exercising them according to its own wise, prudent, and just discretion. Its duty is not only to restore those States, but also to make sure of a lasting peace, of its own ultimate safety, and the permanent establishment of the rights of all its subjects. To this end, I venture the opinion that the Government of the United States ought to require the people of those States to reform their Constitutions, —

*First.* Guaranteeing to the people of color, now the wards of the Nation, their civil rights as men and women, on an equality with the white population, by amendments irrepealable in terms.

*Second.* Regulating the elective franchise according to certain laws of universal application, and not by rules merely arbitrary, capricious, and personal.

*Third.* Annulling the ordinances of secession.

*Fourth.* Disaffirming the Rebel Debt, and —

*Fifth.* To ratify the anti-slavery amendment of the United States Constitution by their legislatures.

And I would have all these questions, save the fifth — the disposition of which is regulated by the Federal Constitution — put to the vote of the *People* themselves. We should neither be satisfied with the action of the conventions which have been held, nor with what is termed the " loyal vote." We want the *popular* vote. And the rebel vote is better than the loyal vote, if on the right side. If it is not on the right side, then, I fear, those States are incapable at present of reorganization ; the proper power of the Union Government is not restored ; the people of those States are not yet prepared to assume their original functions with safety to the Union ; and the state of war still exists ; for they are contumacious and disobedient to the just demands of the Union, disowning the just conditions precedent to reorganization.

We are desirous of their reorganization, and to end the use of the war power. But I am confident we cannot reorganize political society with any proper security : *First.* Unless we let in the *people* to a coöperation, and not merely an arbitrarily selected portion of them ; *Second.* Unless we give those who are, by their intelligence and character, the natural leaders of the people, and who surely will lead them by and by, an opportunity to lead them now.

I am aware that it has been a favorite dogma in many quarters, "*No Rebel Voters.*" But it is impossible in certain States to have *any* voting by white men, if only "loyal men" — *i. e.*, those who continued so during the rebellion — are permitted to vote. This proposition is so clear that the President adopted the expedient of assuming that those who had not risen above certain civil or military grades in the rebel public service, and who had neither inherited nor earned more than a certain amount of property, should be deemed and taken to be sufficiently harmless to be intrusted with the suffrage in the work of reorganization. Although there is some reason for assuming that the less conspicuous and less wealthy classes of men had less to do than their more towering neighbors in conducting the States into the Rebellion and through it, still I do not imagine that either wealth or conspicuous position, which are only the accidents of men, or, at most, only external incidents, affect the substance of their characters. I think that the poorer and less significant men who voted, or fought, for "Southern Independence" had quite as little love for "the Yankees," quite as much prejudice against "the Abolitionists," quite as much contempt for the ₐcolored man, and quite as much disloyalty at heart, as their more powerful neigh-

12

bors. The true question is, now, not of past disloyalty, but of present loyal purpose. We need not try to disguise the fact that we have passed through a *great popular Revolution.* Everybody in the Rebel States was disloyal, with exceptions too few and too far between to comprise a loyal force sufficient to constitute the State even now that the armies of the Rebellion are overthrown. Do not let us deceive ourselves. The truth is, the public opinion of the white race in the South was in favor of the rebellion. The colored people sympathized with the Union cause. To the extent of their intelligence, they understood that the success of the South meant their continued slavery; that an easy success of the North meant leaving slavery just where we found it; that the *War* meant — if it lasted long enough — their emancipation. The whites went to war and supported the war, because they hoped to succeed in it; since they wanted, or thought they wanted, separation from the Union, or "Southern Independence." There were, then, three great interests. There were the Southern whites, who, as a body, wished for what they called "Southern Independence;" the Southern blacks, who desired emancipation; the people of the "loyal States," who desired to maintain the constitutional rights and the territo-

rial integrity of the Nation. Some of us in the
North had a strong hope, which, by the favor of
God, has not been disappointed, out of our defense
of the Union to accomplish the deliverance of our
fellow-men in bondage. But the " *loyal* " *idea*
included emancipation, not for its own sake, but
for the sake of the Union — if the Union could
be saved, or served, by it. There were many men
in the South — besides those known as loyal —
who did not like to incur the responsibility of war
against the Union ; or who did not think that the
opportune moment had arrived to fight " the
North ;" or in whose hearts there was " a divided allegiance." But they were not the positive men. They were, with very few exceptions,
not the leading minds, the courageous men, the
impressive and powerful characters ; they were
not the young and active men ; and when the
decisive hour came, they went to the wall. No
matter what they thought, or how they felt, about
it ; they could not stand or they would not stand
— certainly they did not stand — against the
storm. The Revolution either converted them,
or swept them off their feet. Their own sons
volunteered. They became involved in all the
work and in all the consequences of the war.
The Southern People — as a People — fought,
toiled, endured, and persevered, with a courage,

a unanimity and a persistency not outdone by any people in any Revolution. There was never an acre of territory abandoned to the Union while it could be held by arms. There was never a rebel regiment surrendered to the Union arms until resistance was overcome by force, or a surrender was compelled by the stress of battle or of military strategy. The people of the South, men and women, soldiers and civilians, volunteers and conscripts, in the army and at home, followed the fortunes of the Rebellion and obeyed its leaders, so long as it had any fortunes or any leaders. Their young men marched up to the cannon's mouth, a thousand times, where they were mowed down like grain by the reapers when the harvest is ripe. Some men had the faculty and the faith in the Rebel cause, to become its leaders. The others had the faculty and the faith to follow them. All honor to the loyal few ! But I do not regard the distinction between loyal and disloyal persons of the white race residing in the South during the rebellion, as being, for present purposes, a practical distinction. It is even doubtful whether the comparatively loyal few, with certain prominent and honorable exceptions, can be well discriminated from the disloyal mass. And, since the President finds himself obliged to let in the great mass of the disloyal, by the very terms of his proclamation of amnesty, to a participation in the business of reorganizing the Rebel States, I am obliged also to confess that I think to make one rule for the richer and higher rebels, and another rule for the poorer and more lowly rebels, is impolitic and unphilosophical. I find evidence, in the granting of pardons, that such also is the opinion of the President.

When the day arrives, which must surely come, when an amnesty substantially universal shall be proclaimed, the leading minds of the South, who by temporary policy and artificial rules had been, for the while, disfranchised, will resume their influence and their sway. The capacity of leadership is a gift, not a device. They whose courage, talents, and will, entitle them to lead, will lead. And these men, not then estopped by their own consent or participation, in the business of reorganization, may not be slow to question the validity of great public transactions enacted during their own disfranchisement. If it is asked, in reply, " What can they do ? " and " What can come of their discontent ? " I answer, that while I do not know just what they can do, nor what may come of it, neither do I know what they may not attempt, nor what they may not accomplish. I only know that we ought to demand, and to

secure, the coöperation of the strongest and
ablest minds and natural leaders of opinion in
the South.   If we cannot gain their support of
the just measures needful for the work of safe
reorganization, reorganization will be delusive and
full of danger.

Why not try them? They are the most
hopeful subjects to deal with, in the very nature
of the case.   They have the brain and the experience and the education to enable them to understand the exigencies of the present situation.
They have the courage, as well as the skill, to
lead the people in the direction their judgments
point, in spite of their own and the popular
prejudice.   Weaker men, those of less experience, who have less hold on the public confidence, are comparatively powerless.   Is it consistent with reason and our knowledge of human
nature, to believe the masses of Southern men
able to face about, to turn their backs on those
they have trusted and followed, and to adopt the
lead of those who have no magnetic hold on their
hearts or minds?   Reorganization in the South
demands the aid of men of great moral courage,
who can renounce their own past opinions, and
do it boldly; who can comprehend what the
work is, and what are the logical consequences
of the new situation; men who have interests

urging them to rise to the height of the occasion. They are not the strong men, from whom weak, vacillating counsels come ; nor are they the great men, from whom come counsels born of prejudices and follies, having their root in an institution they know to be dead, and buried beyond the hope of resurrection.

Has it never occurred to us all, that we are now proposing the most wonderful and unprece-. dented of human transactions ?  The conquering government, at the close of a great war, is about restoring to the conquered rebels not only their local governments in the States, but their representative share in the General Government of the country !  They are, in their States, to govern themselves as they did before the rebellion.  The conquered rebels are, in the Union, to help govern and control the conquering loyalists !  These being the privileges which they are to enjoy when reorganization becomes complete, I declare that I know not any safeguard, precaution, or act of prudence, which wise statesmanship might not recognize to be reasonable and just.  If we have no right to demand guarantees for the future ; if we have no right to insist upon significant acts of loyal submission from the rebel leaders themselves ; if we have no right to demand the positive popular vote in

favor of the guarantees we need ; if we may not
stipulate for the recognition of the just rights of
the slaves, whom, in the act of suppressing the
rebellion, we converted from slaves into freemen,
then I declare that we had no right to emanci-
pate the slaves, or to suppress the rebellion.

It may be asked : Why not demand the suffrage for colored men, in season for their vote in
the business of reorganization ?    My answer is,
I assume that the colored men are in favor of
those measures which the Union needs to have
adopted.    But it would be idle to reorganize
those States by the colored vote.    If the popular
vote of the white race is not to be had in favor
of the guarantees justly required, then I am in
favor of holding on just where we now are.    I
am not in favor of a surrender of the present
rights of the Union to a struggle between a
white minority aided by the freedmen on the one
hand, against a majority of the white race on the
other.    I would not consent, having rescued
those States by arms from secession and rebellion, to turn them over to anarchy and chaos.
I have, however, no doubt, none whatever, of
our *right* to stipulate for colored suffrage.    The
question is one of statesmanship, not a question
of constitutional limitation.

If it is urged that the suffrage question is one

peculiarly for the States, I reply: So also that of the abolition of slavery ordinarily would have been. But we are not now deciding what a loyal State, acting in its constitutional sphere, and in its normal relations to the Union, may do; but what a rebel, belligerent, conquered State must do, in order to be reorganized and to get back into those relations. And in deciding this, I must repeat that we are to be governed only by justice, humanity, the public safety, and our duty to reorganize those conquered, belligerent States, as we can and when we can, consistently therewith.

In dealing with those States, with a view to fulfilling the national guarantee of a republican form of government, it is plain, since the nation is called upon to reorganize government, where no loyal republican State Government is in existence, that it must, of absolute necessity, deal directly with the People themselves. If a State Government were menaced and in danger of subversion, then the Nation would be called upon to aid the existing government of the State in sustaining itself against the impending danger. But the present case is a different one. The State Government was subverted in each Rebel State more than four years ago. The State, in its corporate capacity, went into rebellion, and,

as long as it had the power, waged and maintained against the Nation rebellious war. There
is no Government in them to deal with. But
there are the People. It is to the people we
must go. It is through their people alone, and
it is in their primary capacity alone, as people
unorganized and without a government, that the
Nation is capable now of dealing with them at
all. And, therefore, the Government of the
Nation is obliged, by the sheer necessity of the
case, to know who are the people of the State,
in the sense of the National Constitution, in order to know how to reach them. Congress, discerning new people, with new rights and new
duties and new interests (of the nation itself
even) springing from them, may rightfully stipulate in their behalf. If Congress perceives
that it cannot fulfill its guarantee to all the people
of a State, without such a stipulation, then it
not only may, but it ought to, require and secure
it. The guarantee is one concerning *all*, not
merely a *part* of the *People*. And, though the
Government of a State might be of republican
form, and yet not enfranchise its colored citizens;
still the substance and equity of the guarantee
would be violated, if, in addition to their non-
enfranchisement, the colored people should be
compelled to share the burdens of a State Gov-

ernment, the benefits of which would enure to
other classes, to their own exclusion.

A republican form of government is not of
necessity just and good. Nor is another form,
of necessity, unjust and bad. A monarch may
be humane, thoughtful, and just to every class
and to every man. A republic may be inhuman, regardless of, and unjust to, some of its
subjects. Our National Government and most
of the State Governments were so, to those
whom they treated as slaves, or whose servitude
they aggravated by their legislation in the interest of slavery. The Nation cannot hereafter
pretend that it has kept its promise and fulfilled
its guarantee, when it shall have only organized
governments of republican *form*, unless it can
look all the *people* in the face, and declare that it
has kept its promise with them all. The voting
class alone — those who possessed the franchise
under the State Constitutions — were not the
*People.* They never were THE PEOPLE. They
are not now. They were simply the *trustees*
of a certain power, for the benefit of *all* the people, and not merely for their own advantage.
The Nation does not fulfill its guarantee by dealing with them alone. It may deal through
them, with the people. It may accept their action as satisfactory, in its discretion. But, no

matter who may be the agents, through whom
the Nation reaches and deals with the people,
that guaranty of the National Constitution is
fatally violated, unless the nation secures to *all
the people* of those disorganized States the substantial benefits and advantages of A GOVERN-
MENT.   We cannot hide behind a *word*.   We
cannot be content with the "*form*."   The *substance* bargained for is a *Government*.   The
" form " is also bargained for, but that is only
an incident.   The *people*, and *all the people alike*,
must have and enjoy the benefits and advantages
of a *government*, for the common good, the just
and equal protection of each and all.

But, What of the policy of the President ?
I am not able to consider his future policy.   It
is undisclosed.   He seems to me to have left to
Congress alone the questions controlling the
conditions on which the Rebel States shall resume
their representative power in the Federal Government.   It was not incumbent on the President to do otherwise.   He naturally leaves the
duty of theoretical reasoning to those whose responsibility it is to reach the just practical conclusion.   Thus far the President has simply
used, according to his proper discretion, the
power of commander-in-chief.   What method he
should observe was a question of discretion, in

the absence of any positive law, to be answered by himself. He might have assumed, in the absence of positive law — during the process of reorganization — purely military methods. Had that been needful, it would have been appropriate. If not necessary, then it would have been unjust and injurious. It is not just to oppress even an enemy, merely because we have the power. In a case like the present, it would be extremely impolitic, and injurious to the nation itself. Bear in mind, ours is not a conquest by barbarians, nor by despots; but by Christians and republicans. The commander-in-chief was bound to govern with a view to promoting the true restoration of the *power* of the Union, as I attempted to describe it in the beginning of this address; not merely with a view to the present, immediate control of the daily conduct of the people. He deemed it wise, therefore, to resort to the democratic principle, to use the analogies of republicanism and of constitutional liberty. He had the power to govern through magistrates under military or under civil titles. He could employ the agencies of popular and of representative assemblies. Their authority has its source, however, in his own war powers as commander-in-chief. If the peace of society, the rights of the government,

and of all its subjects, are duly maintained, then
the method may justify itself by its success as
well as its intention.  If he has assisted the
people to reorganize their legislatures, and to
reëstablish the machinery of local State government; though his method may be less regular
than if an Act of Congress had prescribed it,
still it has permitted the people to feel their way
back into the works and ways of loyalty, to ex-
hibit their temper of mind, and to "show their
hands."   Was it not better for the cause of free
government, of civil liberty, to incur the risk of
error in that direction, than of error in the opposite one ?   It has proved that the National Government is not drunk with power ; that its four
years' exercise of the dangerous rights of war
has not affected its brain.   It has shown that the
danger of despotic centralism, or of central
despotism, is safely over.

Meanwhile, notwithstanding the transmission
of the seals to State magistrates chosen by vote
in the States themselves ; notwithstanding the
inauguration, in fact, of local legislatures, the
powers of war remain.   The commander-in-chief
has not abdicated.   His generals continue in the
field.   They still exercise military functions, according to the belligerent rights of the nation.
What the commander-in-chief may hereafter do,

whether less or more, depends, I presume, in great measure on what the people of the Rebel States may do or forbear doing. I assume that, until the executive and legislative departments of the National Government shall have reached the *united* conclusion that the objects of the *war* have been fully accomplished, the national declaration of *peace* is not and cannot be made.

The proceedings already had are only certain acts in the great drama of reorganization. They do not go for nothing; they were not unnecessary; nor do I approach them with criticism. But they are not the whole drama. Other acts are required for its completion. What they shall be, depends in part on the wisdom of Congress to determine.

The doctrine of the President that, in the steps preliminary to reorganizing a State which is not, and has not been, theoretically cut off from the Union, he must recognize its own organic law antecedent to the rebellion, need not be contested. I adhere, quite as strictly as he, to the logical consequences of that doctrine. I agree that the Rebel States ought to come back again into the exercise of their State functions and the enjoyment of their representative power, by the action and by the votes of the same class of persons, namely, the same body of voters, or tenants of political rights and privileges, by the votes, action or submission of whom those States were carried into the Rebellion. But yet it may be, at the same time, needful and proper, in the sense of wise statesmanship, to require of them the amplification of certain privileges, the recognition of certain rights, the establishment of certain institutions, the redistribution even of political power, — to be by them accorded and executed through constitutional amendments, or otherwise, — as elements of acceptable reorganization, and as necessary to the readjustment of political society in harmony with the new relations and the new basis of universal freedom resulting from the Rebellion itself. If these things are found to be required by wise statesmanship, then the right to exact them, as conditions of restoring those States to the enjoyment of their normal functions, is to be found just where the Nation found the right to crush the Rebellion and the incidental right of emancipating slaves.

Now, distinctions between men as to their rights, purely arbitrary and not founded in reason or in the nature of things, are not wise, statesmanlike, or "republican" in the constitutional sense. If they ever are wise and statesmanlike, they become so only where oligarchies, privileged orders and hereditary aristocracies are wise and expedient. There are two kinds of republican government, however, known to political science, namely, aristocratic republics and democratic republics : or those in which the government resides with a few persons, or with a privileged body, and those in which it is the Government of the People. I cannot doubt that nearly all men are prepared to admit that our governments, both State and National, are constitutionally democratic, representative republics. That theory of government is expressly set forth in the Declaration of Independence. The popular theory of government is again declared in the preamble to the Federal Constitution. The Federal Government is elaborately constructed according to the theory of popular and representative government, and against the aristocratic theory, in its distinguishing features ; and, in divers places, the Federal Constitution, in set terms, presupposes the democratic and representative character of the governments of the States, for example, by assuming that they have legislatures, that their legislatures are composed of more than one body, and by aiming to prevent even all appearance of aristocratic form by prohibiting the States from granting any title of nobility. In his recent message to Congress, President Johnson affirms " the great distinguishing principle of the recognition

13

of the *rights of man*," as the fundamental idea in all our governments. " The American system," he adds, in the same paragraph, " rests on the assertion of the *equal right* of every man to life, liberty, and the pursuit of happiness, to freedom of conscience, to the culture and exercise of all his faculties." But, is it pretended that the idea of a Government of the People, and for the People, in the American sense, is inclusive of the white race only, or is exclusive of men of African descent ? On what ground can the position rest ?

The citizenship of free men of color, even in those States where no provision of law seemed to include them in the category of voters, has been frequently demonstrated, not only as a legal right, but as a right asserted and enjoyed. Nay more ; both under the Confederation, and at the time of the adoption of the Constitution of the United States, all free native born inhabitants of the States of New Hampshire, Massachusetts, New York, New Jersey, and North Carolina, though descended from African slaves, were not only citizens of those States, but such of them as had the other necessary qualifications, possessed the franchise of electors on equal terms with other citizens. And even Virginia declares, in her ancient Bill of Rights, " that all men having sufficient evidence of permanent common interest with, and attachment to, the community, have the right of suffrage." Wherever free colored men were recognized as free citizens or subjects, but were, nevertheless, not fully enfranchised, I think that the explanation is found, not in the fact of their mere color, nor in their antecedent servitude, but in the idea of their possible lapse into servitude again, of which condition their color was a badge and a continuing presumption. The policy of some States seems to have demanded that slavery should be the prevailing condition of all their inhabitants of African descent. In those States, the possession of freedom by a colored man has therefore been treated as if that condition was only exceptional and transient. But, wherever the policy and legislation of a State were originally dictated by men who saw through the confusion of ideas occasioned by the presence of slavery, there we are enabled to discern the evidence of an unclouded purpose (with which the American mind always intended to be consistent), namely: *The maintenance of equality between free citizens concerning civil* RIGHTS, *and the distribution of* PRIVILEGES *according to capacity and desert and not according to the accidents of birth.* And now that slavery has been rendered forever impossible within any State or Territory of the

Union, by framing the great natural law of Universal Freedom into the organic law of the Union, all the ancient disabilities which slavery had made apparently attendant on African descent, must disappear.

Whatever may be the rules regulating the distribution of political power among free citizens, in the organization of such a republican government as that guaranteed by the National Constitution, *descent* is neither the evidence of right, nor the ground of disfranchisement. The selection of a fraction or class of the great body of freemen in the Civil State, to be permanently invested with its entire political power, — (selected by mere human predestination, irrespective of merit), — that power to be incommunicable to the freemen of another class, — the two classes, of rulers and ruled, governors and governed, to be determined by the accident of birth, and all the consequences of that accident to descend by generation to their children, — seems to me to be the establishment of an hereditary aristocracy of birth, the creation of a privileged order, inconsistent both with the substance and the essential form of American republicanism, unstatesmanlike and unwise; and (in the Rebel States) in every sense dangerous and unjust.

To demand a certain qualification of intelligence is eminently safe, and consists with the interests and rights of all. It is as reasonable as to require a certain maturity of age. They who are the representatives of the political power of society, acting not only for themselves, but also for the women and children, who too belong to it ; representing the interests of the wives, mothers, sisters, daughters, infant sons, and the posterity of us all, ought to constitute an audience reasonably competent to hear. And, since the congregation of American voters is numbered by millions, and covers a continent, it cannot hear with its ears all that it needs to know; but must learn intelligently much that it needs to know, through the printed page and by means of its eyes. The protection of the mass of men against the deceptions of local demagogues, and against their own prejudices hereafter, as well as the common safety, calls for the requirement of the capacity to read the mother tongue, as a condition of coming for the first time to the ballot-box. Let this be required at the South, and immediately the whole Southern community will be aroused to the absolute necessity of demanding free schools and popular education. These are, more than all things else, to be coveted, both for the preservation of public liberty, and for the temporal salvation of the toiling masses of our own Saxon and

Norman blood, whom, alike with the African slave, the oppression of ages has involved in a common disaster.

I think that the wisest and most intelligent persons in the South are not ignorant of the importance of raising the standard of intelligence among voters; and of extending the right to vote so as to include those who are of competent intellect, notwithstanding the recent disability of color. There is evidence that they are not unwilling to act consistently with the understanding, example, and constitutional precedents of the fathers of the Republic; consistently with the ancient practice of the States, coeval with the organic law of the nation, established by the very men who made that law, who used and adopted the very phrase, " a republican form of government," of the meaning of which their own practice was a contemporary interpretation. But if the conquering power of the Nation, if the victorious arm of the Union is paralyzed; if the Federal Government, standing behind the ramparts of defensive war, wielding its weapons, both of offense in the hour of struggle, and of diplomacy in the hour of triumph, is utterly powerless to stipulate for the execution of this condition; then I confess I do not know how the best and wisest in the South will be enabled, deserted and alone, to stand up on its behalf against the jealousy of ignorance and the traditions of prejudice.

If the measures which I have attempted to delineate are found to be impracticable, then Congress has still the right to refuse to the Rebel States readmission to the enjoyment of their representative power, until amendments to the Federal Constitution shall have been obtained, adequate to the exigency. Nor can the people of the Rebel States object to the delay. They voluntarily withdrew from Congress ; they themselves elected the attitude of disunion. They broke the agreements of the Constitution : not we. They chose their own time, opportunity and occasion to make war on the Nation, and to repudiate the Union. They certainly cannot now dictate to us the time or the terms. Again, I repeat, the just discretion of the Nation, exercised in good faith towards all, must govern.

The Federal Union was formed, first of all, " *to establish justice.*" " Justice," in the language of statesmen and of jurists, has had a definition, for more than two thousand years, exact, perfect, and well understood.

It is found in the Institutes of Justinian, —

" Constans et perpetua voluntas, jus suum cuique tribuendi."
" The constant and perpetual will to secure TO EVERY MAN HIS OWN RIGHT."

I believe I have shown that under our Federal Constitution, —

1. All the people of the Rebel States must share in the benefits to be derived from the execution of the national guarantee of republican governments ;

2. That *our* " republican form of government " demands " The maintenance of equality between free citizens concerning civil *rights*, and the distribution of *privileges* according to capacity and desert, and not according to the accidents of birth ; "

3. That people " of African descent," not less than people of the white race, are included within the category of free subjects and citizens of the United States ;

4. That, in the distribution of political power, under our form of government, " *descent* is neither the evidence of right, nor the ground of disfranchisement ; " so that

5. The disfranchisement of free citizens, for the cause of " descent," or for any reason other than lawful disqualification, as by non-residence, immaturity, crime, or want of intelligence, violates their constitutional rights ;

6. That, in executing our national guarantee of republican government to the people of the Rebel States, we must secure the constitutional civic liberties and franchises of all the people ;

7. That we have *no right* to omit to secure to the new citizens, made free by the Union, in war, their equality of rights before the law, and their franchises of every sort, including the electoral franchise, according to laws and regulations, of universal, and not of unequal and capricious, application.

We have no right to evade our own duty. We must not, by substituting a new basis for the apportionment of Representatives in Congress, give up the just rights of these citizens. Increasing the proportion of the political power of the loyal States at the expense of the disloyal States, by adopting their relative numbers of *legal voters* instead of their relative *populations*, while it might punish some States for not according the suffrage to colored men, would not be justice to the colored citizen. For *justice* demands, " for every man *his own* right."

Will it be said that, by such means, we shall strengthen our own power in the loyal States, to protect the colored people in the South ? If we will not yield to them *justice* now, on what ground do we expect grace to give them " *protection* " hereafter ? You will have compromised for a consideration, paid in an increase of your own political power, your right to urge their voluntary enfranchisement on the white men of the South. You will have bribed all the elements of political selfishness in the whole country, to combine against negro enfranchisement. The States of the Rebellion will have no less power than ever in the Senate; and the men who hold the privilege of electing representatives to the lower house, will retain their privilege. For the sake of doubling the delegation from South Carolina, do you suppose that the monopoly of choosing three members would be surrendered by the whites, giving to the colored men the chance to choose six? Nay; would the monopolists gain anything by according the suffrage to the colored man, if they could themselves only retain the power to dictate three representatives, and the colored people should dictate the selection of the other three?

The scheme to substitute legal voters, instead of population, as the basis of representation in Congress, will prove a delusion and a snare. By diminishing the representative power of the Southern States, in favor of other States, you will not increase Southern love for the Union. Nor, while Connecticut and Wisconsin refuse the suffrage to men of color, will you be able to convince the South that your amendment was dictated by political principle, and not by political cupidity. You will not diminish any honest apprehension at extending the suffrage, but you will inflame every prejudice and aggravate discontent. Meanwhile, the disfranchised freedman, hated by some because he is black, contemned by some because he has been a slave, feared by some because of the antagonisms of society, is condemned to the condition of a hopeless pariah of a merciless civilization. *In* the community, he is not *of* it. He neither belongs to a master, nor to society. Bodily present in the midst of the society composing the State, he adds nothing to its weight in the political balance of the nation ; and, therefore, he stands in the way, occupies the room, and takes the place, which might be enjoyed as opportunities by a white immigrant who would contribute by his presence to its representative power. Your policy would inflame animosity and aggravate oppression, for at least the lifetime of a generation, before it would open the door to enfranchisement.

Civil society is not an aggregation of individuals. According to the order of nature, and of the Divine economy, it is an aggregation of families. The adult males of the family *vote* because the welfare of the women and children of the family is identical with theirs ; and it is intrusted to their affection and fidelity, whether at the ballot-box or on the battle field. But, while the voting men of a given community represent the welfare of its women and children, they do not represent that of another community. The men, women and children of Massachusetts are alike concerned in the ideas and interests of Massachusetts. But the very theory of representation implies that the ideas and interests of one State are not identical with those of another. On what ground, then, can a State on the Pacific or the Ohio gain preponderance in Congress over New Jersey or Massachusetts· by reason of its greater number of *males*, while it may have even a less number of *people ?* The halls of legislation are the arenas of debate, not of muscular prowess. The intelligence, the opinions, the wishes, and the influence of women, social and domestic, stand for something — for much — in the public affairs of civilized and refined society. I deny the just right of the Government to banish woman from the count. She may not vote, but she thinks ; she persuades her husband : she instructs her son ; and through them, at least, she has a right to be heard in the government. Her existence, and the existence of her children, are to be considered in the State.

No matter who changes ; let Massachusetts,

at least, stand by all the fundamental principles of free, constitutional, republican government.

The President is the tribune of the people. Let him be chosen directly by the popular election. The Senate represents the reserved rights and the equality of the States. Let the Senators continue to be chosen by the Legislatures of the States. The House represents the opinions, interests, and equality of the *people* of each and every State. Let the people of the respective States elect their representatives in numbers proportional to the numbers of their people. And let the legal qualifications of the voters, in the election of President, Vice President, and Representatives in Congress, be fixed by a uniform, equal, democratic, constitutional rule, of universal application. Let this franchise be enjoyed " according to capacity and desert, and not according to the accidents of birth." Congress may, and ought, to initiate an amendment granting the right to vote for President, Vice President and Representatives in Congress, to colored men, in all the States, being citizens and able to read, who would, by the laws of the States where they reside, be competent to vote if they were white. Without disfranchising existing voters, it should apply the qualification to white men also. And the amendment ought to leave the election of President and Vice President directly in the hands of the people, without the intervention of electoral colleges. Then the poorest, humblest, and most despised men, being citizens and competent to read, and thus competent, with reasonable intelligence, to represent others, would find audience through the ballot-box. The President, who is the Grand Tribune of all the People, and the direct delegates of the People in the popular branch of the National Legislature, would feel their influence. This amendment would give efficiency to the one already adopted abolishing Slavery throughout the Union. The two amendments, taken together, would practically accomplish, or enable Congress to fulfill, the whole duty of the nation to those who are now its dependent wards.

I am satisfied that the mass of thinking men at the South accept the present condition of things in good faith ; and I am also satisfied that with the support of a firm policy from the President and Congress, in aid of the efforts of their good faith, and with the help of a conciliatory and generous disposition on the part of the North, especially on the part of those States most identified with the plan of emancipation, the measures needed for permanent and universal welfare can surely be obtained. There ought now to be *a vigorous prosecution of the Peace* — just as vigorous as our recent prosecution of the War. We ought to extend our hands with cordial good-will to meet the proffered hands of the South ; demanding no attitude of humiliation from any ; inflicting no acts of humiliation upon any ; respecting the feelings of the conquered ; — notwithstanding the question of right and wrong between the parties belligerent. We ought, by all the means and instrumentalities of peace ; by all the thrifty methods of industry ; by all the recreative agencies of education and religion ; to help rebuild the waste places and restore order, society, prosperity. Without industry and business there can be no progress. In their absence, civilized man even recedes towards barbarism. Let Massachusetts bear in mind the not unnatural suspicion which the past has engendered. I trust that she is able — filled with emotions of boundless joy, and gratitude to Almighty God who has given such victory and such honor to the Right — to exercise faith in His goodness, without vain glory ; and to exercise charity, without weakness, towards those who have held the attitude of her enemies.

The offense of War has met its appropriate punishment by the hand of *War*. In this hour of triumph, honor and religion alike forbid one

act, one word, of vengeance or resentment.
Patriotism and Christianity unite the arguments
of earthly welfare, and the motives of heavenly
inspiration, to persuade us to put off all jealousy
and all fear, and to move forward as citizens and
as men, in the work of social and economic reorganization, each one doing with his might whatever his hand findeth to do.

We might wish that it were possible for Massachusetts justly to avoid her part in the work
of *political* reorganization.     But, in spite of
whatever misunderstanding of her purpose or
character, she must abide her destiny.     She is a
part of the Nation.     The Nation, for its own
ends and its own advantage, as a measure of war,
took out of the hands of the masters, their slaves.
It holds them therefore, in its hands, as freedmen.
It must place them somewhere.     It must dispose
of them somehow.     It cannot delegate the trust.
It has no right to drop them, to desert them.
For, by its own voluntary act, it assumed their
guardianship and all its attendant responsibilities,
before the present generation, and all the coming
generations, of mankind.     I know not how well,
or how ill, they might be treated by the people
of the States where they reside.     I only know
that there is a point beyond which the Nation
has no right to incur any hazard.     And, while

the fidelity of the Nation need not abridge the humanity of the States ; on the other hand our confidence in those States cannot be pleaded before the bar of God, or of history, in defense of any neglect of our own duty. Let their people remember that Massachusetts has never deceived them. To her ideas of duty and her theory of the Government, she has been faithful. If they were ever misled or betrayed by others into the snare of attempted secession, and the risks of war, her trumpet at least gave no uncertain sound. She has fulfilled her engagements in the past, and she intends to fulfill them in the future. She knows that the reorganization of the States in rebellion carries with it consequences which come home to the firesides and the consciences of her own children ; for, as citizens of the Union, they become liable to assume the defense of those governments, when reorganized, against every menace, whether of foreign invasion or of domestic violence. Her bayonets may be invoked to put down insurgents of whatever color, and whatever the cause, whether rightful or wrongful, which may have moved their discontent. And, when they are called for, they will march. If she were capable of evading her duty now, she would be capable of violating her obligations hereafter. If she is anxious to prevent grave

14

errors, it is because she appreciates, from her past experience, the danger of admitting such errors into the structure of government. She is watchful against them now, because, in the sincere fidelity of her purpose, she is made keenly alive to the duties of the present, by contemplating the inevitable responsibilities of the future. In sympathy with the heart and hope of the nation, she will abide by her faith. Undisturbed by the impatient, undismayed by delay, "with malice towards none, with charity for all ; with firmness in the right, as God gives us to see the right," she will persevere. Impartial, Democratic, Constitutional Liberty is invincible. The rights of human nature are sacred ; maintained by confessors, and heroes, and martyrs ; reposing on the sure foundation of the commandments of God.

> " Through plots and counterplots;
> Through gain and loss; through glory and disgrace;
> Along the plains where passionate Discord rears
> Eternal Babel; still the holy stream
> Of *human happiness* glides on!
> .    .    .    .    .    .    .
> There is ONE above
> Sways the harmonious mystery of the world."

*Gentlemen :* For all the favors, unmerited and unmeasured, which I have enjoyed from the people of Massachusetts ; from the councillors, magistrates, and officers by whom I have been surrounded in the government ; and from the members of five successive legislatures ; there is no return in my power to render, but the sincere acknowledgments of a grateful heart.

88 30 8

CPSIA information can be obtained
at www.ICGtesting.com
Printed in the USA
BVHW041519160819
556068BV00022B/2606/P